T0311739

Cambridge Elements ≡

Elements in Religion and Monotheism
edited by
Paul K. Moser
Loyola University Chicago
Chad Meister
*Affiliate Scholar, Ansari Institute for Global Engagement with Religion,
University of Notre Dame*

MONOTHEISM AND THE SUFFERING OF ANIMALS IN NATURE

Christopher Southgate
University of Exeter

CAMBRIDGE
UNIVERSITY PRESS

CAMBRIDGE
UNIVERSITY PRESS

Shaftesbury Road, Cambridge CB2 8EA, United Kingdom

One Liberty Plaza, 20th Floor, New York, NY 10006, USA

477 Williamstown Road, Port Melbourne, VIC 3207, Australia

314–321, 3rd Floor, Plot 3, Splendor Forum, Jasola District Centre, New Delhi – 110025, India

103 Penang Road, #05–06/07, Visioncrest Commercial, Singapore 238467

Cambridge University Press is part of Cambridge University Press & Assessment, a department of the University of Cambridge.

We share the University's mission to contribute to society through the pursuit of education, learning and research at the highest international levels of excellence.

www.cambridge.org
Information on this title: www.cambridge.org/9781108948685

DOI: 10.1017/9781108953092

First published 2023

A catalogue record for this publication is available from the British Library.

ISBN 978-1-108-94868-5 Paperback
ISSN 2631-3014 (online)
ISSN 2631-3006 (print)

Monotheism and the Suffering of Animals in Nature

Elements in Religion and Monotheism

DOI: 10.1017/9781108953092
First published online: June 2023

Christopher Southgate
University of Exeter

Author for correspondence: Christopher Southgate, c.c.b.southgate@ex.ac.uk

Abstract: This Element concerns itself with a particular aspect of the problem posed to monotheistic religious thought by suffering, namely the suffering of non-human creatures in nature. It makes some comparisons between Judaism, Christianity, and Islam, and then explores the problem in depth within Christian thought. After clarification of the nature of the problem, the Element considers a range of possible responses, including those based on a fall-event, those based on freedom of process, and those hypothesising a constraint on the possibilities for God as creator. Proposals based on the motif of self-emptying are evaluated. Two other aspects of the question concern God's providential relationship to the evolving creation, and the possibility of resurrection lives for animals. After consideration of the possibility of combining different explanations, the Element ends its discussion by looking at two innovative proposals at the cutting edge of the debate.

Keywords: suffering, animals, theodicy, evolution, Christianity

ISBNs: 9781108948685 (PB), 9781108953092 (OC)
ISSNs: 2631-3014 (online), 2631-3006 (print)

Contents

Introduction

The fact of suffering poses a problem for believers in a good and loving God. This Element concerns itself with a particular aspect of that problem, namely the suffering of non-human creatures, and a particular sub-division of theistic faiths, the great monotheisms. The problem of suffering for theistic faiths is simply expressed, often as a 'trilemma':

(1) God is perfectly good, just and benevolent, and perfectly aware of the state of every creature.
(2) God has the power to prevent harms and suffering in God's creatures.
(3) These harms and sufferings (often called in the literature 'evils') nevertheless exist.

This classic tension can be resolved by denying the reality of (3), or by commuting either the benevolence or the power of God, or by presenting an argument as to why a benevolent God might not exercise the power in (2).

We are concerned in this study with non-human suffering. Human beings are animals, but for simplicity I will use 'animal' in this Element to refer to 'non-human animals', and again as a form of shorthand I include in this category any non-human creature capable of suffering (which might (arguably) include fish, birds, molluscs, etc.[1]).

After some initial comments in Section 1 about how Judaism, Christianity, and Islam approach the problem of suffering in their scriptures and tradition, the book focusses on Christian thought. The choice, in the early Christian centuries, to adopt the doctrine of *creatio ex nihilo*, God's creation of every not-God existent out of absolutely nothing, intensifies God's apparent responsibility for creaturely suffering and sharpens the problem in view.

Section 2 seeks to clarify the problem, addressing first the objection of neo-Cartesians, who deny the reality of animal suffering. This counter-intuitive claim is examined and set aside. The question as to whether biological extinction is itself an 'evil' is explored – this could be argued either way.

Section 3 explores the nature of theodicies, strategies in Christian thought for addressing the problem of suffering. It distinguishes between philosophical arguments addressing the overall plausibility of Christian theism, which aim at an imagined atheist reader, and arguments within the framework of Christian theology, aimed at puzzling out the difficulties for the believer posed by the problem of evil. The emphasis of this Element is on this puzzling out. Many strategies involve a balancing of goods and harms, and we introduce a way of distinguishing three ways of doing this balancing.

---

[1] On the issue of the possible suffering of fish, see Mason and Lavery 2022.

Section 4 offers a few classic moves in the Christian tradition in respect of the suffering of animals, and then turns to Darwin's theory of evolution by natural selection. Darwinism sees competition and struggle, with its resultant suffering and extinction, as a driver of the refinement of adaptation in creatures, leading to an intensification of the theological problem, if God has seemed to use suffering as a means to an end. I also consider whether an emphasis on cooperation in evolution might mitigate this problem.

In Sections 5–7 I present the three classic theodical strategies for addressing how God set up the world. Section 5 explores the possibility that some fall-event distorted this set-up and resulted in a world containing both beauty and violence. There are proposals that this fall was of the first humans (which the chronology of suffering in evolution seems to make impossible), of rebellious angels, or of a more mysterious kind. All these proposals suffer from the problem that, scientifically, it is the same processes that give rise to violence, struggle, and suffering that give rise to beauty, ingenuity, and complexity in ecosystems.

Section 6 summarises the possibility of a theodicy based on process metaphysics, derived from Whitehead, and also arguments based on freedom of physical processes and of creatures. In such arguments the 'good' of the freedom is used to balance the harms that arise. Whereas in the 'only-way' argument, evaluated in Section 7, God is constrained, in that evolution, with its inevitable element of struggle and suffering, is seen to be the only way to give rise to a biosphere which develops the types of values we see in this world.

Section 8 explores whether the theological theme of self-emptying, kenosis, can be used to generate an evolutionary theodicy. Section 9 then looks at the somewhat neglected question of God's ongoing, providential involvement with an evolving world. This includes consideration of God's possible co-suffering with the sufferings of animals. Another significant element in many theodicies of animal suffering is some form of redeemed, post-mortem existence for animals, and this is explored in Section 10, both in terms of existence in the mind of God, and various proposals for a resurrected life for animals.

A number of writers want to suggest that only a combination of strategies can result in a cogent account of God in the face of animal suffering, so Section 11 looks at some of these compound theodicies and their different approaches. Finally in Sections 12 and 13 I present two innovative proposals that might take the field forward. The first uses resources from Plato's *Timaeus* to amplify the only-way argument; the second explores whether that argument could be combined with a form of the rebellious-angels fall-based theodicy.

One terminological point: Holmes Rolston introduced the term 'disvalues' to cover the aspects of the natural world that seem to argue against its goodness.

His careful analysis repays close study (Rolston 1992). I adopt this helpful term here, and clarify in Sections 2 and 4 exactly what I see the relevant disvalues as being.

It is striking how much energy has emerged in the last fifteen years on this somewhat neglected question. In terms of philosophical approaches, the reader is directed to the monographs of Murray (2008), Dougherty (2014), and Schneider (2020). For more theological treatments, good starting points are Southgate (2008) and Sollereder (2019); see also Hoggard Creegan (2013).[2]

Theoretical treatments of the problem of suffering, as opposed to practical responses, are in general somewhat out of fashion. They have been subjected to sharp criticism by, for example, Surin (1986) and Tilley (1991). But this subject, which is as concerned with flesh ripped from prey by sabre-toothed predators a million years ago as with the present day, and is therefore not about specific interventions to relieve suffering, does lend itself to a theoretical treatment. I hope the reader will gain richly from this brief summary of a rapidly developing field.

1 Monotheism and Suffering

In this section I make some brief comparisons between what are usually termed the three great monotheisms: Judaism, Christianity, and Islam. The rest of the Element will focus on Christian responses to the problem of suffering in non-human animals, that being my area of specific expertise. There are many common emphases in these three faiths, which are explored in John Bowker's classic study *Problems of Suffering in Religions of the World* (Bowker 1970).[3] Alas, Bowker makes hardly any reference to the suffering of non-human animals. He points out however that all three religions address in their Scriptures 'the actual facts of suffering ... Suffering is a part of what it means to be alive' (1970: 101). These Scriptures are not concerned with theoretical discussions of the classic trilemma outlined in the Introduction. Nor are they concerned to prove the existence of God in the face of suffering.

In his opening essay on Judaism, Bowker points out that central to the biblical faith of Israel was that God had acted to deliver the people from slavery, and that that same God had made a series of covenants with the people, establishing a relationship of mutual obligation in which God takes the initiative. (Strikingly,

---

[2] A short summary of the field like this Element cannot treat all the rapidly expanding literature in this area. I have focussed instead on the key sources that will enable readers to explore the field for themselves. Those with access to the journal *Zygon* may also be interested to read the collection of essays in Volume 53(3) for September 2018.

[3] I use Bowker for his exceptional clarity and breadth of learning, aware of the limitations of using a Christian writer to represent other faiths.

the first of these covenants, canonically, is that with Noah at Genesis 6 and 9. In the latter passage the covenant includes 'every living creature that is with you, the birds, the domestic animals, and every animal of the earth with you, as many as came out of the ark' (Gen. 9.10).[4] God's undertaking is not that animals will not suffer, or die, or indeed tear each other apart, but that God will not destroy 'all flesh' from 'the face of the earth'.)

In Judaism too we see the emergence of the radical monotheism that (arguably) reaches its quintessence in Islam.[5] Writing of the prophet Deutero-Isaiah (Is. 40–55), Bowker says this:

> In face of the idea that the world is a battle-ground between the forces of light and the autonomous forces of darkness, Deutero-Isaiah asserted that God creates both light and darkness, weal and woe (Bowker 1970: 8–9).

This biblical faith does not seek to explain the existence of suffering. Rather, '[t]he problem in Scripture is not why suffering exists, but why it afflicts some people and not others. The problem is not the *fact* of suffering but its *distribution*.' (9) Explanations within the Hebrew Scriptures included suffering as a punishment for sin, and as a test, to enable the people to form a more durable relationship with God. Deutero-Isaiah makes another extraordinary move, writing in the enigmatic passages on the Suffering Servant of the redemptive value of suffering (a theme that became of central importance in Christian reflection on Jesus). None of these moves seems to transfer easily to the suffering of non-human animals.

The Hebrew Bible's meditation on suffering culminates in the fable-like story of Job, a righteous, God-fearing, specimen human being who suffers almost unimaginable personal tragedy and protests robustly to God, rejecting the conventional theodicies of the time. God's answer 'from the whirlwind' in Job 38–41 decentres human experience and sets it within a cosmic frame. This emphasis on a vast perspective, to which humans have minimal access, was later developed within Christianity in the theodicy of Augustine (see Section 4).

Very late in the formation of the Hebrew Bible a belief in life after death, not just for martyrs but more generally for the righteous, develops, and this continued to be explored in later writings such as the Books of Maccabees and Enoch. We shall see that this belief forms an important element in many Christian theodicies of non-human animal suffering.

---

[4] All biblical quotations are from the New Revised Standard Version unless otherwise specified.

[5] Though see Kenney (2019) for a reminder that a form of monotheism also emerges out of the Platonic tradition.

In relation to Islam and suffering Bowker writes that: 'What is at issue is the omnipotence of God, and it is made repeatedly clear in the Quran that suffering can only be understood by being contained within that omnipotence' (1970: 102). Even when an angelic agent, Iblis, is understood as the proximate cause of humans' distress 'it is God, after all, who gave respite to Iblis in the first place, and thus allowed his activity.' (105) The teaching that God is the author of weal and woe alike 'is frequently repeated' (119n1). There is a clarity in this Islamic scheme from which Christian theodicists could learn much. But the question remains as to why God should permit all this creaturely suffering. Again two of the same answers – punishment for sin and testing of faith – emerge that we saw in Judaism. Testing is 'a constant and repeated theme of the Quran' (109). Bowker continues, 'The Quran opts firmly for the theory of instrumentality – for the belief that suffering is an instrument of the purposes of God.' (112)

However, this overriding emphasis on the sovereignty of God does leave questions that have been wrestled over throughout the history of Islam, as to what place can be given to freedom of creaturely action. Although this Element is not concerned with humans, their freedom or their suffering, the idea that there is freedom in the actions of non-human creatures, and possibly in physical processes, will be important to our later discussions. This tension between divine control and creaturely freedom is explored by Keith Ward in his inter-faith exploration *Religion and Creation* (Ward 1996). Taking as indicative of new directions in twentieth-century Islamic theology the work of Mohammed Iqbal, Ward explains that for Iqbal creative freedom is a profound good, and 'God chooses to create beings who can share in this creativity, realising their own potential within the growing organic unity which is the universe' (1996: 73). In this world 'God does not directly desire us to suffer exactly as we do. God has decreed that we shall exist in a world in which such suffering may come upon us.' (74)

So in these brief comments on monotheisms other than Christianity, a map is already developing of possibilities. God may be taken to directly determine all events, or set a pattern to events to realise divine purposes, in which case the responsibility for suffering would seem to remain with God. Or God may, while remaining sovereign, award a greater degree of freedom to creatures, from the exercise of which freedom suffering may arise. In such a case responsibility may be shared between God and creatures. At the far end of the latter case lies the theology of the post-Holocaust Jewish philosopher Hans Jonas, who wrote:

> ... in order that the world might be and be for itself, God renounced his own being, divesting himself of his deity – to receive it back from the Odyssey of time weighted with the chance harvest of unforeseeable temporal experience:

transfigured or possibly even disfigured by it. In such self-forfeiture of divine integrity for the sake of unprejudiced becoming, no other foreknowledge can be admitted than that of possibilities which cosmic being offers in its own terms: to these, God committed his cause in effacing himself for the world (Jonas 1996: 134)

In this scheme God hands Godself over to the world, emptying Godself of power and control. Suffering is (by implication) an inevitable part of this 'unprejudiced becoming'. As Rabbi Shai Cherry shows, this Jewish theological move has antecedents in the theology of divine self-withdrawal in Isaac Luria, and beyond that in the hiddenness of God motif in the Hebrew Bible (Cherry 2011). Luria has also influenced Christian theologians in dialogue with science such as John Haught and Jürgen Moltmann. Note, however, the *deliberate* handing-over of Godself in this scheme. This builds on the motif of self-emptying that comes into Christianity through reflection on 'the mind that was in Christ Jesus' (Phil. 2), and which is explored in Section 8. It is importantly different from a process-metaphysical scheme in which God's experience is eternally and necessarily embroiled with that of the world (see e.g. Barbour 2001, and Section 6).

Far more could be said about theodicies in Judaism and Islam, but I turn for the rest of this Element to how Christian thinkers have approached the specific problem of the suffering of non-human animals. Early Christianity inherited both the monotheism of ancient Israel and that emerging from the Platonic tradition (so Kenney 2019). Beyond that, orthodox Christianity from the late second Century CE held increasingly that God had created everything out of nothing. So not only was there no counter-deity opposing God from eternity, but there was no primordial 'stuff' constraining God's possibilities of enacting God's purposes in creation (such as Plato had postulated in the *Timaeus*).[6]

The doctrine of creation out of nothing therefore exacerbated the problem of harms and suffering in the natural world. *Creatio ex nihilo* has come under vigorous scrutiny in recent years, on biblical (May 1994), feminist (e.g. Keller 2003), and ethical grounds (Bauman 2009). For recent surveys of the status of *creatio ex nihilo* see Burrell *et al.* 2010; Oord (ed.) 2015; Anderson and Bockmuehl (2018). The doctrine is rejected on metaphysical grounds by many process theologians. The critique that concerns us here is the theodical – the charge that *creatio ex nihilo* puts the blame for the disvalues of natural evil so squarely on the shoulders of God as to be inconsistent with a continued claim as to the absolute benevolence of God. This is a charge levelled especially by

---

[6] But see Section 12 for a scheme incorporating themes from the *Timaeus* within a Christian framework.

Oord (2015). Nevertheless, *creatio ex nihilo* remains the orthodoxy in much Christian systematic theology. Vitally, this type of theology can insist both on God's utter transcendence from the world, and at the same time the intimate relation of the Creator to all creatures.[7]

I note also that orthodox versions of the monotheisms do not allow for reincarnation of humans as animals (or vice versa). So a defence of the morality of animal suffering based on karma is not available to these faiths.

I now turn to the exercise of clarifying exactly what the problem is that theology might address.

2 Clarifying the Problem

In this section I seek to identify exactly what, in the lives of non-human animals, constitutes the problem requiring theological attention. J. R. Illingworth, writing in the important collection of Anglican essays *Lux Mundi* could say:

> The universality of pain throughout the range of the animal world, reaching back into the distant ages of geology, and involved in the very structure of the animal organism, is without doubt among the most serious problems which the Theist has to face. (Illingworth 1890: 113)

This is a striking quotation, showing the importance this subject gained in the decades after Darwin. But Illingworth is not in my view correct. The experience of pain is a very important biological response, enabling creatures which possess that experience to detect a noxious stimulus, assess its severity, and seek to avoid it. The primary issue with which we are concerned here is not pain but suffering. I reflected on this issue in my book *The Groaning of Creation*, as follows:

> Wesley J. Wildman has made an important effort to clarify terminology in this field. He chooses the term 'suffering' to cover everything from physical injury to a biological organism through 'conscious pain' to 'emotional distress' and 'existential anxiety'. Wildman is helpful in clarifying why we should not impute suffering either to a 'dying' star, or yet to an ecosystem as a whole. He concludes rightly that suffering 'can only exist in the context of intensely structured, biochemically regulated forms of being'. (Wildman 2007: 56)

I continued:

> However, I do not share his sense that the term 'suffering' is a neutral word well suited to covering the range of meanings he asks of it. I think injury takes place in many organisms without pain being experienced – insects may well

---

[7] See Kathryn Tanner (2005: Ch. 2) on 'non-contrastive transcendence'.

> be an example (see DeGrazia 1996: Ch. 5) and pain where it is experienced
> may be momentary, succeeded either by relief (or by death). I would not
> regard such situations as necessarily involving *suffering*. Suffering seems to
> me to belong only to situations of intense pain, particularly where no relief is
> in sight, and prolonged distress, physical or psychic. (Southgate 2008: 136,
> n15, references modified)

Non-human creatures may not carry around with them an awareness of death as
humans do, but many of them know the experience of acute pain, and when that
pain comes with no avenue of relief, it seems to me that it constitutes not merely
a useful physiological response, but actual suffering. Animals may not know the
experience of existential dread, but higher animals know what it is to be trapped,
to lose their freedom of action – observation of zoo animals alone tells us that. In
the wild this type of suffering comes as they are cornered by predators, or
succumb to disease or injury. I understand suffering to occur when animals with
the capacity to feel pain experience it in an intense, or chronic, way from which
no release can be obtained. This suffering I take to be a charge against the
goodness of God as creator. Animals may also suffer if competition destroys
their reproductive opportunities, or excludes them from a social group.

The Objection of Neo-Cartesians

Before going further into the problem for theists, and Christian theologians,
occasioned by reflection on the suffering of animals in nature, it is important to
acknowledge the so-called 'neo-Cartesian' view that this suffering does not in
fact exist. (The name refers to Descartes' famous and infamous view that
animals can be viewed as automata.) The most prominent recent examples are
a chapter in C. S. Lewis's *The Problem of Pain* (1962) and an influential article
by Peter Harrison (1989). Harrison's claim is that animals cannot be regarded as
feeling pain, because they lack 'continuity of experience'. By this he means that

> there is nothing [by way of continuity of identity] to which that pain can
> belong. The animal and, dare I say it, the neonate, have no self and their pains
> are rather successive states which lack the connexion that would render them
> 'painful experiences' (Harrison 1989: 90–1).

Murray devotes a whole chapter to neo-Cartesianism. He notes that most readers
will find this hard to credit, but 'the evidence against the neo-Cartesian position is
quite weak' (Murray 2008: 71). Although pain-detection systems are widespread,
humans have two such systems – a 'discriminative' pathway 'which discerns the
'cognitive features' of the stimulus (location, intensity, duration, etc.)', and an
'affective' pathway 'which accounts for the unpleasant feeling or 'painful' part of
nociception' (67). In human beings the latter pathway 'terminates in the prefrontal

cortex, a region of the mammalian brain which was the last to evolve (and so occurs only in humanoid primates)' (68).

A recent contribution to the debate has come from Jon Garvey in his 2019 book *God's Good Earth: The Case for an Unfallen Creation*.[8] As Garvey is a medical doctor who has specialised in the neurophysiology of (human) back pain, his views on the suffering of non-human creatures are important. And he offers some useful analysis, pointing out that pain responses are confined to less than 5 per cent of all species. Indeed he goes on to claim that 'we are left with only a tiny proportion (much less than 1 percent) of all living species that appear even theoretically capable of experiencing agony, or even significant suffering' (Garvey 2019: 159). Only in the larger animals, according to Garvey, do responses to harm constitute pain. We might cautiously accept this (with a possible demur about his assessment of molluscs, given recent research into the sophistication of responses in octopi[9]).

Garvey observes that we would expect evolved predation to be highly efficient. He also makes a significant point that 'shock anaesthesia' may greatly reduce the distress of the prey animal (162). This is important – an animal in fight or flight mode may not experience as much pain or integrated awareness of their plight as their wounds might suggest. Garvey is also interesting on parasitism, which he notes as very common in insects and (however ugly it appeared to Darwin) pain-free. Garvey continues, 'there is no clear demarcation line between parasitism, commensalism in which the organism does no harm to its host) and symbiosis (in which host and symbiont benefit each other)' (157).

At the same time it is impossible for this author to avoid the conclusion that Garvey has tidied up the evolutionary narrative to suit his theological point (that creation is unfallen). Surprisingly, he rejects the consensus view that the vast proportion of species that have ever lived are now extinct – this apparently on the basis of a radically 'punctuated' view of evolution. But this seems at variance with Garvey's general point about predatory strategies as having been refined to minimise struggle. That point would seem to rely on long processes of gradual refinement, rather than sudden development of innovation as in a punctuated view. Moreover, a major element in the problem of evolutionary suffering rests on the perception that harm-causing strategies did evolve from less efficiently adapted behaviours, and that struggle and attendant suffering were among the drivers of refined characteristics (see Section 4).

---

[8] Perhaps it is not entirely accurate to say that he has joined the debate, since he makes no reference to any recent theological contributions other than that of Russell (2008).

[9] See the film 'My Octopus Teacher', a 2020 Netflix Original documentary directed by Pippa Ehrlich and James Reed.

Also, however much Garvey might celebrate parasitism in insects, he does not comment on the very evident chronic distress it can cause in many larger animals. There is evidence that such chronic parasitism occurred in dinosaurs (see Schneider 2020: 41). And this distress is presumably not ameliorated by shock anaesthesia.

Garvey is suspicious of the images of violence and struggle depicted in wildlife films, which he regards as edited, or even staged, to provide a kind of 'nature porn' (2019: 160). One could wish that he had engaged with the work of a lifelong naturalist like Holmes Rolston (cf. Rolston 1986, 1988). Garvey, Rolston, and I find common ground in affirming the wonderful and God-breathed, God-sustained character of the natural world. But it is hard to avoid the conclusion that Garvey has over-minimised the ambiguities of God's 'very good' creation to serve his point. A recent nature documentary chronicled the starvation to death of two young lions who had become detached from their group. They called plaintively for help, and up ahead the pride were calling, but out of earshot. The camera crew, so far from seizing on nature porn, eventually found themselves unable to continue filming what cannot but be thought of as a case of chronic suffering.

I am the first to acknowledge that there are dimensions to human suffering to which there is no non-human parallel – to do with memory, and anticipation of painful experiences, and with the complexities of the human psyche interacting with culture. No other animal knows the shame of being trolled on the internet, or the dread of the redundancy notice, or the ache of the anniversary of a loved one's death. I also acknowledge that our knowledge of the minds of other animals is profoundly limited. But I find the analysis of Schneider persuasive (2020: 56–64; cf. also Dougherty 2014: 61–4). Schneider points out first that 'the *appearance* of animal suffering is extremely strong' (2020: 59); those who work intimately with animals tend to have a strong sense of the reality of their capacity to suffer. Second, he questions 'even if animals do exist subjectively in a continuous present tense … how does this mode of temporality reduce the moral badness of their pain?' (61).

Schneider also notes that a neo-Cartesian view is convenient to those supporting industrial farming and experimentation on animals. I wonder in contrast whether our collective guilt over these practices may not intensify our tendency to anthropomorphise animal experience. But unquestionably the general trend in animal studies tends to reduce the differences between human capacities and those of other animals, and to take animal experiences more and more seriously (cf. Clough 2012). So with the caveats of Garvey noted, I set aside the neo-Cartesian claim that the lack of second-order reflection on their first-order responses to their environment implies that distress in other animals is not a moral disvalue.

Beyond the actual experience of animals, there is a further dimension to the question of the character of the natural world as created, and that is the aesthetic. Even if we were to accept a neo-Cartesian analysis, such as that of Harrison, that animals do not suffer, are not moral victims, the Christian thinker might still question whether this is a fitting world for God to have created. In Darwin's famous example of the ichneumon wasp, whose larvae eat their host caterpillar alive as they mature, it is the ugliness of the strategy that may disturb even someone who has been convinced that the caterpillar cannot feel pain.

Well, the biologist might reply that that shows that our aesthetics are distorted. We project our feelings onto the host, failing to notice the ingenuity of the parasitic strategy. Indeed in earlier writing I have suggested that the ingenuity of the life cycle of the malarial parasite might be taken as a sign of the ingenuity of the Creator (Southgate 2018a: 143–4).[10] In this way of thinking what is far from beautiful may nevertheless speak of glory. But Schneider makes an important point when he calls for an evolutionary theodicy that is able to 'help people to "see" divinity in the Darwinian World in a non-wishful, affectively authentic intuitive fashion' (2020: 45). For a satisfactory Christian theology of creation there need to be positive theological inferences from the natural world as we now understand it, not merely endless defences. Also, the theodicist must consider the difficulty that the witness of Christ to the radically self-giving character of God seems at variance with an understanding of God as having created a world based on ruthless self-preservation.

Much turns on the divine verdict on creation in Genesis 1. Four times what emerges from the divine creative word is called 'good' (*tōv* in Hebrew), and at 1.31 the whole is summarised as 'very good'. It is important to realise that *tōv* does not have the same connotations of beauty or aesthetic perfection as the Greek *kalos*, which is normally used to translate *tōv*. The Hebrew has much more the connotation of fitness for purpose than beauty or perfection (cf. Rogerson 1991). However in the Christian tradition there is much appeal to the goodness of creation as associated with beauty. So where we see behaviours that strike us as profoundly ugly, they will be a challenge to our theistic seeing.

Another Aspect of the Problem – the Question of Extinction

It is generally thought (*pace* Garvey) that over 99 per cent of species that have ever existed are now extinct. Is this a problem for the theological evaluation of creation as good? I am not considering here anthropogenic extinction, caused by human activity, but those extinctions that occur through the operation of the evolutionary process in the non-human world. Some argue that extinction is

---

[10] But see Section 13 for an alternative reading of parasitism.

a natural process and not necessarily a disvalue (see e.g. McFarland 2014: 77). I am less clear on this. Some of the aspects of possible animal suffering I listed above – loss of reproductive opportunities, and of social opportunities for flourishing – would apply to the last individuals of some species (the last of the 'hobbit-like' hominin *Homo Floresiensis* for example). And extinction may result in loss of ecosystemic richness (in other species that cooperated with or depended on the species in question), though equally it may provide new opportunities, new niches.

We might also ask why we so lament the extinction of species in the present day. Is this simply for their instrumental value to humans – as something for our children and grandchildren to experience (or exploit)? Or do we recognise any extinction as an irreversible loss of a whole way of being alive in God's creation, and a loss of a particular song of creaturely praise to God?[11] On balance I am inclined to think that the extent of non-anthropogenic extinction over evolutionary time, the loss of so many ways of being alive, is a disvalue, an aspect of the problem an evolutionary theodicy must tackle.

In Section 3 I consider general methodologies for tackling the problem of suffering in Christian thought, and in Section 4 I explore some responses of pre-Darwinian Christian writers, and explain how Darwin's own scheme intensifies the problem.

3 Applying Approaches to the Problem of Evil to Animal Suffering

A valuable summary of approaches to the problem of suffering can be found in the introduction to Adams and Adams (1990). A common terminology is that of 'evil' or 'evils', which is misleading because the word is ordinarily associated with wickedness. The problem is better expressed as one of harms to creatures and the suffering they cause, but we are stuck with the language the literature uses. 'Moral evil' refers to harms committed by morally aware freely choosing creatures; 'natural evil' covers all other instances of harms and suffering.

This Element is concerned with the suffering of (non-human) animals in nature. Therefore it does not engage with human cruelty to animals, or ecological harms caused by human folly. The problem we address here may therefore be taken to be part of the problem of natural evil – how the character of the natural world causes harms and suffering to creatures. In a monotheistic religion, in which divinity is not divided between benevolent and malefic deities, the suffering of animals in nature must be presumed, in the first instance, to be the responsibility of God. We shall consider various attempts to draw the

---

[11] On the theme of creaturely praise, see Southgate 2018a: 131–4, and references therein.

sting of this responsibility. They include ascribing the underlying cause of the suffering to a primordial human sin, or to the rebellion of angels (see Section 5). Such ascriptions cause the problem to revert to one of moral evil.

But we start with the problem posed by the existence of creaturely harms and suffering to the monotheistic 'God of the philosophers' – the one God considered to be perfect in power, knowledge, and benevolence. Adams and Adams provide a formal statement of the problem, as follows:

Is 'God exists, and is omnipotent, omniscient, and perfectly good' consistent with the existence of evils?
More precisely, if:
    (P1) A perfectly good being would always eliminate evil so far as it could;
    (P2) An omniscient being would know all about evils;
    and
    (P3) There are no *limits* to what an omnipotent being can do.

(Adams and Adams 1990: 2)

then P1–P3 seem inconsistent with the existence of evils.

Atheological Approaches and Philosophical Defences

Importantly, there are two significantly different types of approaches to this problem. The first is in Adams and Adams' language 'atheological' (1990: 3). The inconsistency outlined here is used by atheist thinkers to challenge the plausibility of theism. So Paul Draper argues that the apparent absence of design in a Darwinian universe goes better with a godless world of natural selection than with a theistic world (Draper 2012). One of the most famous, and incisive, of these atheological arguments is that of William Rowe, first published in 1979 (Rowe 1990). Rowe concedes that no atheists can establish a full logical inconsistency between the existence of God and the existence of evils. He accepts Alvin Plantinga's argument against such a *logical* inconsistency (Plantinga 1974). But Rowe is confident he can show an *evidential* inconsistency that undermines the plausibility of theism. He deploys his well-known example of a fawn trapped in a lightning-caused forest fire. The fawn dies in horrible lingering agony. Rowe points out that 'there does not appear to be any greater good such that the prevention of the fawn's suffering would require either the loss of that good or the occurrence of an evil equally bad or worse.' (Rowe 1990: 130). The Cambridge Element on *The Problem of Evil* in the Philosophy of Religion series by Tooley (2019) concludes on analytic grounds that the suffering of non-human creatures provides a compelling case that God does not exist (2019: Ch. 2).

There are philosophical thinkers whose primary concern is to address questions that non-human suffering raises for the plausibility of theism. Thus, their arguments are explicitly or implicitly addressed to atheist objections to such plausibility. The form of these arguments is often as analytic defence of the possibility that creaturely suffering is compatible with the classical attributes of God, especially omnipotence and omnibenevolence. On a small canvas a good example is the essay by Michael Rota in *Evolution, Games and God* (Rota 2013). Having questioned whether we can have an answer to the question 'why would God bother to use an evolutionary process at all?' (2013: 364) Rota offers a brief analysis suggesting that for God to confer on creation 'the dignity of causality' and to maintain divine hiddenness might be reasons why.

An important example of a philosophical defence of the compatibility of theism with suffering in non-human animals is Lecture 7 of Peter van Inwagen's carefully crafted Gifford Lectures of 2003 (van Inwagen 2006). The form of van Inwagen's argument is interesting. He holds that '[the theist] is required to show only that *for all anyone knows* this judgment is correct' (2006: 120). Or to put it another way, the theist need only provide 'a story according to which God and suffering . . . both exist, and which is such that . . . there is no reason to think that it is false, a story that is not surprising on the hypothesis that God exists' (van Inwagen 1995: 74).

Still the best survey of these philosophical arguments is Michael Murray's 2008 monograph *Nature Red in Tooth and Claw*. Murray advances a number of possible explanations for 'evolutionary evil'. His objective is to discover whether any of these explanations is an adequate defence of the goodness of God in the face of the fact of non-human suffering. He considers that even van Inwagen's criterion is too demanding. Murray points out that 'the task of deflecting the evidential worries raised by evil can look quite different depending on one's starting point' (2008: 39). He looks for arguments that can count, in effect, as character witnesses for God in the face of suffering. He calls each of these a *causa Dei* (40).

Interestingly, Murray goes on to claim that only a composite of several arguments will constitute a sound defence of the goodness of God (see Section 11). So his eventual conclusions are congruent with the more theological theodicy I presented in *The Groaning of Creation* (Southgate 2008), and we shall encounter several of them as we explore the problem.

These defences of theism may also draw on classic arguments in philosophical theodicy. So Trent Dougherty in *The Problem of Animal Pain* wants to show that the 'Irenaean' approach advanced by John Hick – whereby creatures learn or develop properties that God desires through processes that involve suffering – can be applied to suffering in evolution. This is a challenging task, as Hick himself realised (Hick 1966: 345–53), both because we know so little about the inner life of animals, but also because individual animals are often not in a position to learn from the harms that they experience – their suffering is followed by death, rather than the development of character, or yet virtue.

I have a fundamental concern about Dougherty's methodology. He wants to substitute for strict deductive reasoning the use of an evidential approach to probability. He wants, then, to use probability and application of Bayes' Theorem to compare the weight of theories. I am never easy when precise mathematical methods are imported into other conceptual frameworks, in which the precise value of probabilities can never be known. When Dougherty writes, 'the theist must show not only that evil doesn't count against theism, but that it is at least as probable on theism as on naturalism' (Dougherty 2014: 100) I find it hard to know how such probability could be calculated (or yet whether there exists a neutral standpoint from which the calculation could be made).

More promisingly, Dougherty follows Marilyn McCord Adams in adopting Roderick Chisholm's requirement that theodicies do not merely balance off evils, but 'defeat' them. Adams offers two versions of this defeat in the eventual (eschatological) perspective of the sufferer:

> [R]etrospectively, from the vantage point of the end of the journey, the person one eventually becomes would be glad to have made the sacrifice [of being a participant in the horror]. Participation in horrors can thus be integrated into that overall development that gives positive meaning to his or her life, and so be defeated within the context of the individual's existence as a whole.
>
> Retrospectively, I believe, from the vantage point of heavenly beatitude, the victims of horrors will recognise those experiences as points of identification with the crucified God, and not wish them away from their life histories. (Both passages as quoted in Dougherty 2014: 114.)

Dougherty, rightly in my view, prefers the second formulation. It is hard to see a Holocaust survivor being 'glad' of the experience, even considered from a vast distance of eschatological reflection. But both these defeats require powers of cognitive reflection not usually associated with animals other than humans. Dougherty proposes that these powers are conferred after death. I discuss this move, which is found (somewhat differently) also in Schneider and Sollereder, in Section 10.

John R. Schneider's *Animal Suffering and the Darwinian Problem of Evil* (2020) continues the tradition of applying the techniques of philosophy of religion to the question that concerns us. Schneider's diagnosis of Darwinism's contribution to the problem (see Section 4) is helpful, even if he misses a key point about teleology. He is admirably clear that the usual efforts to deflect responsibility for evolutionary suffering from God will not work. And interestingly he is sceptical of whether any of the classic theodical approaches can work on the problem. Instead he also sides with Chisholm. He is in search not, like Murray, of a *causa Dei* but of a 'defeater'. Evils are to be 'defeated by being incorporated into a larger, greatly good whole' (205). For Schneider this involves mounting an aesthetic theodicy. What is to be set against the fact of creaturely harms is a broader contemplation of the artistry of the Creator, in a way that Schneider hopes will enable a recovery of 'theistic seeing' (45). This aesthetic argument, based on God as Artist, leads Schneider into more theological territory. He draws first on the motif of kenosis. This is a development of the claim, in Phil. 2.7, that Christ 'emptied himself, taking the form of a servant'. This much-explored text is the basis for a broader understanding of self-giving as central to the Christ-event. Encouraged by the work of Holmes Rolston, Schneider sees a form of kenosis as threaded through the Darwinian narrative. (For more on this, see Section 8.) Second he proposes a form of post-death existence for animals, which we will consider in Section 10. I evaluate these theological moves in later sections. For now I would merely observe that God subjecting myriad creatures to involuntary suffering remains profoundly troubling, however powerful an appeal is made to the beauty of the overall whole.

Andrew Ter Ern Loke places a strong reliance on scriptural arguments, so his work is not typical of these defences. Nevertheless his explicit desire to address the challenge posed by evils to the plausibility of Christian theism places him in the category we have been discussing. Loke, like Murray, wants to keep open a whole range of possible explanations of evolutionary evil – the wrong choices of angels, which may have perturbed the delicately balanced initial conditions of creation; free choices in creatures; the failure of angels and humans to exert their God-given vocation to 'subdue' the non-human world; and the possibility of life after death for non-human animals (Loke 2022: Ch. 4). I can make nothing of the penultimate suggestion. There is no evidence for angels being given a vocation to subdue the created world, and a human vocation to subdue creation (itself identified as deeply problematic by many ecotheologians) could not have affected the vast bulk of creaturely suffering over evolutionary time. I evaluate the other options in Sections 6 and 10.

Aporetic Arguments and Theological Theodicies

Adams and Adams contrast this atheological approach with what they term 'aporetic' approaches (1990: 2). This is a helpful term for approaches in which the apparent inconsistency between God's goodness and the existence of evils generates a theological aporia or puzzle. For the Christian theodicist, this puzzle invites a deeper exploration within the framework of Christian thought, and a possible nuancing of propositions within that framework. To my mind, the aim of this nuancing is to generate a least-worst version of the framework, for adoption by worshipping communities in the face of the fact of creaturely harms and suffering, and so to enhance understanding of a God whose ways with the world remain ultimately mysterious.

The contrast between this theological work and the philosophical defences outlined above is well illustrated by, on the one hand, Rota's 'if God exists, why did he bother to use an evolutionary process at all' (2013: 364) compared with Sarah Coakley's starting point in the essay that follows his: 'God, the Holy Spirit, is the perpetual invitation and lure of the creation to return to the Father, yet never without the full – and suffering – implications of incarnate sonship' (Coakley 2013: 378).

The rest of this Element is not addressed to the atheist seeking to undermine the plausibility of theism. I am not at all convinced that any arguments shift philosophical atheists to theism or vice versa. My interest is not in whether a particular argument is a logical possibility to be brandished at an atheist, but rather whether that argument, taken together with other reflections on Scripture, tradition, reason, and experience, advances our understanding of the God confessed in Christ.

Karen Kilby provides a good example of this more theological approach to theodicy. She writes:

> there are three features of a Christian theology, all of which are desirable, but not all of which can be achieved; a theology ought to provide a fully Christian picture of God; it ought to give, or at least leave room for, a full recognition of the injustice, terror and tragedy that we participate in and see around us; it ought to be clear that it hangs together (Kilby 2020: 81–2)

Kilby herself is willing to sacrifice the third to the other two, and to regard systematic theology as therefore 'systematically dissonant' (81). Indeed any theodical exploration must acknowledge its limits. Theodicy as I wrote years ago 'arises out of protest and ends in mystery' (Southgate 2008: 132).

Good-Harm Analyses

Despite my preference for exploring issues of suffering aporetically, as a theological puzzle rather than a formal philosophical trilemma, there is a taxonomic move of a semi-philosophical character that Andrew Robinson and I published some years ago and which is valuable in the precise classification of theodical approaches (Southgate and Robinson 2007).

We note that most theodicies find some way of relating some good or goods to the acknowledged harms that present the problem. We divide this relating into three main types:

(i) property-consequence good-harm analyses, in which the presence of a property that may be deemed good has a likely consequence of a range of harms. The classic example is the free-will defence against moral evil. The possibility of self-conscious freely choosing action informed by an understanding of other creatures, in a creature such as a human, is taken to be so great a good as to balance the very many harms that may arise from the use of that freedom.

(ii) developmental good-harm analyses, in which a process through which various types of value develop may also lead to disvalues. These may arise as a by-product of the value-generating process, or they may be instrumental in furthering the generation of value. An example of a harm as a by-product would be the exhaustion of a runner on a training programme towards a marathon run for charity. The exhaustion is not an instrument of stamina development but a likely by-product. An example of an instrumental system would be a student assessment scheme with severe penalties for plagiarism or excessive word-count. The harms, or possibility of harms, are instrumental to the development of the habits of a good scholar.

(iii) constitutive good-harm analyses, in which the good is inseparable from the harm. This most elusive and enigmatic possibility can be glimpsed in the experience of some human sufferers that only in and through their suffering did a certain closeness to God become possible. (Southgate 2018b: 296–7)

When Murray affirms the possibility that freely chosen rebellion by angels is the reason for evolutionary evil, he sides with a property-consequence type of argument (Murray 2008: 96–101, 103–6). The God-conferred freedom had the possible consequence of great harms to mortal creatures. Whereas Nancey Murphy explicitly identifies suffering as a by-product of the characteristics of the evolutionary process that develop the attributes of creatures; she therefore offers a developmental by-product analysis (Murphy 2007). It will be seen that 'Irenaean' theodical strategies, which rely on the development of creaturely properties, fall into the developmental category, whereas an Augustinian scheme, based on the use and abuse of the property of freedom, would fall into the property-consequence category. We shall encounter versions of all these strategies when we turn to the more overtly theological responses to the suffering of non-human creatures.

4 Theodical Moves in the Christian Tradition, and the Challenge of Darwinism

We shall discuss in the next section what John Polkinghorne describes as 'the ancient Christian answer' (2009: 31) that disvalues in nature must be attributed to the sin of the first humans. But in this section we consider other moves found in important thinkers in the tradition. I then explore the impact on the problem of animal suffering of Darwin's theory of evolution by natural selection.

Piet Slootweg has provided a catalogue of theodicies of non-human suffering through the centuries. It is important to remember the context of writing of different theologians. A willingness to blame God for the predicament of creatures is apparent in the psalms of lament in the Hebrew Bible, but is foreign to Augustine, who writes: 'we must not venture to blame the work of such a maker [i.e. the Creator] in any respect through the temerity of human vanity (Augustine, *City of God* XII.4, quoted in Kenney 2019: 102). Augustine's main concern is to encourage souls' faithful contemplation of a God who is pure goodness and cannot be in error, not to 'justify the ways of God to men', in Milton's famous phrase. Context is very important in considering these premodern positions. Aquinas in the thirteenth century CE is not doing exactly what Irenaeus is attempting in the second, and Leibniz in the eighteenth century is attempting something different again.[12]

With these caveats, however, we can note the importance of these moves:

First, although Irenaeus of Lyons is inclined to attribute predation among animals to Adam's disobedience (Slootweg 2022: 31), he is important for introducing an understanding of the creation as a place of *development*, admittedly only in his view the development of human beings (Hick 1966: 218–21).

Second, I note Augustine's appeal to an *aesthetic* argument, and to our ignorance of the whole picture, as in this passage:

> Since, then, in those situations where such things were appropriate, some perish to make way for others . . . and the less succumb to the greater . . . this is the appointed order of things transitory. Of this order the beauty does not strike us, because by our mortal frailty we are so involved in a part of it, that we cannot perceive the whole, in which these fragments that offend us are harmonized with the most accurate fitness and beauty. (*City of God* XII.4, quoted in Hick 1966: 92)[13]

---

[12] For further discussion of theologians' approach to the natural world, and hence to natural evil, see McGrath (2016).

[13] See Rosenberg (2018) for an important essay noting that Augustine does not have an over-idealised view of pre-fall nature. He accepts the existence of the poisonous viper and the rot-causing worm (Rosenberg 2018: 237).

Aquinas also deploys an aesthetic argument that:

> the whole itself (. . .) is all the better and more perfect if some things in it can fail in goodness. (. . .) Hence many good things would be taken away if God permitted no evil to exist; for fire would not be generated if air was not corrupted, nor would the life of a lion be preserved unless the ass were killed. (Aquinas 2020: Part 1, Qu. 48, Art. 2, Reply to Objection 3, as quoted in Slootweg 2022: 54)

So, 'Some evils are needed to ensure a greater good. The nature of beasts of prey belong [*sic*] to this category.' (Slootweg 2022: 55) Aquinas, starting from an aesthetic argument about what is most perfect or fitting, develops a property-consequence good-harm analysis, with the 'good' being (his sense of) the perfection of creation.

Hick discusses this sort of position as it has been carried forward in Catholic theology, that 'God merely permits natural evil as the unavoidable concomitant of His achieving some great good', and notes that it is incompatible with what such theologians often also want to insist, namely that God 'could had He wished have created instead a better universe free from those evils' (Hick 1966: 111). So this type of good-harm analysis tends to require some version of Leibniz's conviction that this is 'the best of all possible worlds'.[14]

Leibniz's phrase has been much derided by those engaging with the problem of suffering, especially because it can offer little or no comfort to sufferers. Also philosophers have wanted to be cautious about the terminology of 'the best'. Perhaps the formulation of Robin Attfield is more satisfying to the contemporary ear: 'there are no grounds to hold that a value-loving creator would select for creation a different world from the actual world' (Attfield 2017: 85).

After Slootweg's historical survey, he goes on to assert that Darwin's ideas made no difference to the question of the suffering of non-human animals, as the whole range of solutions had already been canvassed by earlier writers. This surprising claim leads us on to consider Darwin's theory and his own (implicit) theodicy.

I summarise Darwin's theory of evolution by natural selection as follows:

> Darwin saw that variations in biological forms were always arising, some of which could be inherited. Also that typically there are always more members of a species born than can reproduce successfully. He concluded that there will always be competition for resources, and those variants that were better adapted to their environment would give rise to more descendants – those variations would be 'selected for' and other variations would tend to disappear from the population. This is the essence of his theory of 'natural selection', and of its enormous explanatory power. Its implication is plain – less well adapted members of a species will tend to have a shorter life and fewer descendants.

---

[14] For a good summary of Leibniz on the problem of evil, see Murray and Greenberg (2013).

> Further, the success of many species depends on their predating upon other species.[15] The competition to reproduce will drive the characters of species towards greater and greater refinement – and systems of predation will generate excellence in predator and prey alike. (Southgate 2008: 2)

I agree that the bare fact of suffering in a world created by God out of nothing creates a presumption of God's responsibility, and that that presumption is not really affected by Darwinism. But I cannot agree with Slootweg that Darwin's theory makes no difference to the theodicy of non-human suffering, for the following reason. What is most troubling to the Christian believer about the theory of evolution by natural selection is that:

> the suffering of creatures is *instrumental* – it serves God's purposes, if those purposes are to realize more and more sophisticated and better adapted ways of being in the world. 'Darwin's God' seems to *use* natural selection to further those ends, and that means more and more intricate ways of competing with other individuals and predating upon other species. It is the weak, always, who go to the wall in this system, the erratically swimming fish that attracts the shark, the lame antelope calf that is singled out by the hyena pack, the floundering zebra that is seized by the crocodile. (Southgate 2008: 5)

It is interesting to compare this with Schneider's analysis of how Darwinism changed the problem of creaturely suffering (Schneider 2020: Ch. 1). He draws on Darwin's letter to Asa Gray in which Darwin confesses that 'I own I cannot see, as plainly as others do, & as I should wish to do, evidence of design and beneficence on all sides of us' (Darwin 1860). 'Theistic seeing', in Schneider's phrase, becomes more difficult when the creation seems to lack design and evidence of God's love. He goes on to list the following ways in which Darwinian biology has intensified the problem.

First, the discovery of deep evolutionary time, and that 'violence and predation had been features of the nonhuman natural realm from its beginning' (Schneider 2020: 21). Second, evolution has passed through 'a plurality of worlds' (22), and 'this successive creation and destruction of entire animal "worlds" seems to be the product of undirected, random chance . . . it appears, at least, to be dysteleological – lacking in any discernible underlying purpose that we might plausibly ascribe to the design of God' (24). See Section 9 for more discussion. Third, Schneider talks about 'anti-cosmic micro-monsters', strategies that, he claims, exhibit an element of horror that 'exacerbates the tragic character of this realm of discovery' (38). He gives an example from the present, the giant water bug, which reduces its victim's

---

[15] Predation is an excellent strategy for deriving energy from the environment, because in the bodies of organisms the energy comes in an already highly ordered form, together with the essential building-blocks of life (cf. Rolston 1992). So it is no surprise that whole pyramids of predation build up – these are what ecologists term 'food chains'.

body to a juice that it sucks out, and one from the past, in the array of parasites and pathogens postulated to have populated the body of a dinosaur. I am less sure about this element in Schneider's analysis, since after all these phenomena reveal great ingenuity of evolved strategy (for a comment on this in relation to the malarial parasite, see Southgate 2018a: 143–4). So we should be wary of trusting too much to our aesthetic disgust. Fourth, Schneider draws on a sense of evils being 'inscribed' into creation. Quoting Murray's starting point that 'predation, pain and death were now viewed as among the very instruments of creation' (Murray 2008: 2), Schneider faces with refreshing honesty the implication 'that God is the deliberate authorizing agent of evolutionary evils' (Schneider 2020: 43). This is effectively the point I make above about God being responsible not only for the existence of the evils but also for their instrumentality in generating values.

Darwin's own writings make clear that he is aware both of this instrumental point, and of the turmoil it could generate for those attempting theistic seeing. In the famous ending to *The Origin of Species* he celebrates his conclusion that 'from the war of nature, from famine and death, the most exalted object which we are capable of conceiving, the production of the higher animals, directly follows' (Darwin 1859: 425). The instrumental character of disvalues could not be plainer.[16] And Darwin sees how problematic this may be for people of faith: 'what a book a devil's chaplain might write on the clumsy, wasteful, blundering, low and horridly cruel works of nature!' (Darwin 1856).

Evolution Evolving

Darwinian evolution is a robust scientific theory but like all good theories it continues to evolve, undergoing vigorous scrutiny giving rise to extensions (such as the rise of epigenetics) and changes of emphasis. For a very good summary, see Jablonka and Lamb 2014. A number of scholars have proposed that the motifs of competition and struggle have been overstated, and have pointed to the extent of cooperation and symbiosis in ecosystems. Nicola Hoggard Creegan provides a summary of new dynamics in evolutionary theory, which she claims may have 'profound theological consequences' (2013: Ch. 8, quotation on 124–5). Cooperation and its implications for theology are sensitively explored by Sarah Coakley in her 2012 Gifford Lectures (Coakley 2012). She writes:

> The phenomenon of cooperation, seen now to be as deeply inculcated in the propulsion of evolution – from the bacterial level upwards – as Darwin's celebrated principle of mutation and selection, provides a significant modification of the 'nature red in tooth and claw' image that Darwinism early accrued to itself. (Coakley 2013: 382)

---

[16] For a study of Darwin's choices of metaphor and their influence, see Beer 2009.

For Joshua Moritz, shifts of scientific emphasis provide a response to 'the charge that God heartlessly chose to create life predominantly through a mechanism that *intrinsically* relies on and moves forward through competition, selfishness, and bloodshed' (Moritz 2014: 356, italics in original).

I am less convinced by these proposals. Yes, the theologian in this field needs to keep abreast of these scientific debates. Yes, Darwin's theory did not provide any satisfactory account of how novelty arises in genomes or organismic behaviours, and modern understandings of genetic drift and niche construction make important contributions. But it would be wrong to suppose that cooperative strategies necessarily reduce the force of natural selection. In a world of scarce resources, there are always likely to be losers in evolutionary 'games' – cooperation just changes the configuration of the winning strategies. I give as example the recent discovery in my own city of Exeter of previously unsuspected cooperation among peregrine falcons. The effect of this cooperation is a more effective strategy for destroying competing raptors called buzzards (Southgate 2015). Even Moritz concedes that 'Cooperation-oriented models of evolutionary change do not remove the *fact* of particular instances of animal suffering throughout evolutionary history' (Moritz 2014: 356, italics in original). I consider Moritz's own theodicy in Section 6.

This section has indicated some approaches to the suffering of non-human creatures in the tradition, and how and why Darwin's theory transformed the problem. We now turn to efforts to resolve this theological issue, starting with explanations of the suffering based on some form of fall-event.

5 Fall-Event-Based Theodicies

As I noted in Section 1, the combination of monotheism and creation out of nothing places a heavy implicit responsibility for the disvalues in nature on God as creator. This section explores a range of ways in which this responsibility might be mitigated by attributing the disvalues to another agent, a creature or class of creatures that 'falls' from a state of harmony with God.

Human Fall

The classic move in Christian theodicy has been to attribute both moral and natural evil to the fall of the first human couple, drawing on the story in Genesis 3. This first sin was regarded as the source of death, and also the curse on the ground (Gen. 3.17). This scheme was developed to the full by Augustine of Hippo (see Kenney 2019: Ch. 4). It is best understood as a logical inference from a full-hearted embrace of both creation out of nothing and the fundamental goodness of creation (Gen. 1.31). Evil can have no real existence given the goodness of creation; it can only be a dereliction from the good ('*privatio boni*'). Disvalue must therefore result from the free conscious choices of creatures, and Genesis 3 seems the classic locus of such a choice.

This formulation is not unproblematic in itself. First, the rest of the Hebrew Bible does not seem to know this human fall into corruption, or a cursed natural world. The 'Fall' seems to reappear only in the intertestamental literature; it then receives a powerful spur from Paul's formulation of the first and second Adams in Rom. 5. Second, it is not easy to understand the logic of this first human decision, as Schleiermacher demonstrated in his critique of the doctrine (see Pedersen 2020: Ch. 3). Third, as Sollereder shows, it is possible to argue that the curse on the natural world is reversed at Genesis 8.21 (see Sollereder 2019: Ch. 2 for an important analysis).

The greatest obstacle to an understanding of disvalues in the non-human world stemming from a human fall is that the fossil record makes it clear that predation and parasitism, with the suffering these necessarily involve, were present millions of years before human beings themselves evolved. So it is very difficult to see how human sin could have given rise to these phenomena. The one recent effort to retrieve human culpability from this chronological obstacle is found in Dembski (2009). He holds that God imposed suffering proleptically on the non-human creation, knowing humans would fall. Dembski draws an analogy with the retrospective causation often attributed to the salvific effect of the Cross. This argument has been robustly refuted by Michael Lloyd, who points out among other issues (a) the disanalogy between the divine initiative of the atonement and the human sin of disobedience to God and (b) the injustice of God's imposing innocent suffering on creatures so that humans could (later) appreciate their own guilt (Lloyd 2018a: 259–61).

The problems with Dembski's argument illustrate just how bankrupt as a theodicy of evolutionary evil a primordial human sin within historical time must inevitably be. Two possibilities remain within fall-based arguments. There is a neo-Platonic argument dating back to Origen that humans were created first of all as immaterial beings, and only their sinfulness in that state led to their being embodied in a cursed natural world. This notion makes no connection with a scientific understanding of the human being as an evolved animal emerging late in a long process of biological evolution. Nor does it explain why God gave rise not just to cursed humans but to a wider material creation so necessarily infected by this primordial spiritual sin (Murray calls this the 'fragility' objection, see Murray 2008: 82–3).[17]

---

[17] The same objections can be raised to N. P. Williams' notion of the fall of a 'World Soul' (see Murray 2008: 102–3).

That leaves the possibility that the fall was of angels, freely choosing creatures lacking a physical body, and created (presumably) before the arising of the physical universe. The Bible and the tradition contain numerous accounts of angels, and there are a few biblical references to an angelic rebellion (such as Is. 14.12–15; Ezek. 28.12–19; Luke 10.18; Rev. 12.7–12). Gregory Boyd has made much of the spiritual war that he claims resulted. But even Boyd concedes that:

> in sharp contrast to the way chief gods are presented in ANE [Ancient Near Eastern] mythologies, biblical authors uniformly portray Yah-weh as the sole Creator God who never had to fight for his supremacy and whose supremacy is therefore never threatened by anti-creation forces. (Boyd 2017: 1014)

For a critique of Boyd's use of the Bible in relation to natural evil, see Sollereder 2019: 18–19.

Lloyd espouses this angelic-rebellion theodicy, calling in evidence the suggestion of E. L. Mascall that:

> If the lower levels of this cosmos were to be linked together in intimate union …, and if the lower levels of this cosmos were to be under the surveillance and loving care of the higher, it seems reasonable to suppose that defection and rebellion in the angelic realm will drastically disorder the material world (quoted in Lloyd 2018b: 273).

Murray also admits angelic rebellion as a possible theodicy (2008: 103–6). He considers that the fragility objection can be met by presuming that:

> If God structures the world so that there are stable, nomic regularities … creatures who are capable of forming intentions that in turn cause bodily motions will have a great deal of power to affect the natural order … Even a small measure of causal power is sufficient to cause a substantial quantity of evil. (105–6)

Loke makes a related suggestion, that: 'events in the cosmic conflict could have introduced the initial (and scientifically undetectable) perturbations . . . into the dynamical situations which God had created' and goes on to quote Garrett de Weese to the effect that 'continued activity of the demonic horde could, over the history of the world, continue to perturb chaos systems as part of their ongoing campaign against the establishment of the kingdom of God' (Loke 2022: 85).

The merit of this type of argument would seem to be that it seems to preserve the goodness of God, and it is in harmony with Jesus' desire, recorded throughout the Gospels, to confront and reverse disease and death.

I have four concerns about this approach. The first three are theological. I question first: whether the good of according angels the extent of freedom that would enable those angels to inflict the extent of creaturely suffering implied by millions of years of evolutionary struggle is a good outweighing the disvalues. In terms of a good-harm analysis, an angelic fall would be a property-consequence argument, but the property does not, at first sight, appear to justify or outweigh the consequent suffering. Would granting such freedom, presumably knowing its consequences, really be the action of a good God?

Second, I do not see any scriptural evidence for the idea that angels are charged with the 'surveillance and loving care' of the natural world. (Rather key texts in the Hebrew Bible accord this to God in Godself, e.g. at Ps. 104 and Job 38–41.)

Third, proponents of this view accord to the rebelling angels an extent of power over creation that is unfamiliar to the Scriptures and tradition. Lloyd even thinks that the rebelling powers cause biological death.[18] Murray and Loke both seem to imply that the fine balance of a God-ordered creation can be upset by angelic choices, giving rise to the disvalues we see. But an extraordinary extent of power is being presumed, the power to transform the natural world such that it contains creatures predating upon or parasitising other creatures to obtain their energy supplies, which otherwise they would not.[19] This does not speak to me of fine balances being tipped in a God-ordered world but of a major frustration of the presumed will of God. It is, as I have written before, as though God intended to create straw-eating lions, and was unable to do so (Southgate 2011a: 382).

My fourth objection is scientific. It is that what Darwinism teaches us is that the very same processes that give rise to the refinement of creaturely character-istics are the ones that give rise to disvalues. In Rolston's resonant phrase, 'the cougar's fang has carved the limbs of the fleet-footed deer, and vice versa' (Rolston 2006: 134). It is deeply problematic to seek to dissect out biology into beautiful, God-ordered components, and negative elements such as struggle, violence, and even death. A Darwinian picture insists on the unity of these elements.

I shall however return in Section 13 to the possibility of angelic rebellion as a component in an overall theodicy.

Mysterious Fallenness

I now consider three formulations of evolutionary theodicy that absolve God from responsibility for disvalues, but without identifying clearly the source of those disvalues. What arose in creation was not altogether what God willed,

---

[18] Personal communication.

[19] See Rolston (1992) for the benefits of such a 'heterotrophic' world.

although it is not altogether possible to pin down why. For this reason I have called these views 'mysterious fallenness' (Southgate 2018c).

The closest of these views to an angelic rebellion is that of Nicola Hoggard Creegan, for whom the disvalues in creation are like the 'tares' in the parable of the wheat and the tares in the Gospel of Matthew (Mt. 13.24–30 KJV) (Hoggard Creegan 2013; 2018). The appearance of the tares of disvalue is ultimately mysterious. God allows them to co-exist with the values, until the eschaton. But the parable's witness that they are sown by an 'enemy' (Mt. 13.25) suggests that Creegan too invokes a consciously rebellious force.

I also note two ingenious proposals that do not depend on a consciously rebellious agent. The first comes from Neil Messer, invoking Barth's '*Das Nichtige*', nothingness. Messer writes:

> By 'nothingness', [Barth] does not mean 'nothing'. Rather, he means what God rejected, or did not will, when God willed to create all things and declared them 'very good' (Gen. 1.31). As such, nothingness has a strange, paradoxical, negative kind of existence: it is the chaos, disorder or annihilation which threatens God's creation, to which God is implacably opposed, which has been decisively overcome through the work of Christ. My proposal is that some features of the evolutionary process reflect, not God's good creative purpose, but rather nothingness: the disorder and annihilation threatening the goodness of creation. (Messer 2020: 91)

This was Barth's version of *privatio boni*; creation is attended by the possibility of what God does not will. What we know is what God has done in Christ to redeem creation; that for Messer needs to be our emphasis. Celia Deane-Drummond draws on Bulgakov's language of 'Shadow Sophia', the counterpart to the wisdom embedded in creation by the action of the Trinity. She quotes Bulgakov as follows:

> The first action of the Holy Spirit is that in the void of nothing reality arises (in *ouk on* there appears *me on*)[20] . . . This *me on* rages as the elemental power of creation, as "seething chaos" . . . 'the dark face of Sophia". If it is not illuminated, this dark face can even become an opposition to the light, darkness in the process of being actualized, anti-Sophia, the "minus of being". That is why the life of creation is not only an idyll, the blossoming of being, but also the "struggle for existence," the struggle between life and death. (quoted in Deane-Drummond 2018: 803)

The disvalue in the natural world is for Deane-Drummond inevitable rather than necessary. It is 'bound to arise. However, that does not mean that it has to be so

---

[20] Drawing on a distinction in ancient Greek philosophy between absolute absence of being (*ouk on*) and non-being in relation to being (*mē on*).

in an *absolute* sense, even if we cannot in our limited imagination configure this otherwise' (805).

Both Messer and Deane-Drummond invoke a mysterious constraint on the way God's creation turns out. A great deal turns on the nature of this constraint on God's capacity to create a world where there is creaturely flourishing without creaturely struggle, competition, and violence. If the constraint is construed as a spiritual force, then old concerns that exercised the early Christian theologians about dualistic formulations resurface, as Messer himself acknowledges (2020: 90). A God who, from the beginning, has been in a battle with contrary spiritual forces, forces powerful enough to radically transform the character of any creation to which God might give rise, is no longer the sovereign Lord of the cosmos, the God whose ontological priority and absolute goodness guarantees the goodness of creation. If on the other hand the constraint on God's creative action is not an opposing agency but some form of inevitable constraint, how can the inevitability be demonstrated? In the end, these positions have the constraint on God's perfect freedom be a mystery, not a conscious resistance. This type of view seems to me metastable – when the appeal to mystery on which they rest is subject to closer questioning, these approaches would necessarily collapse either into a conscious opposing spiritual force, or a form of logical constraint.

In Section 7 I consider ways of articulating a necessary constraint on God's activity. But first in Section 6 I consider positions in which creation's freedom, intrinsic or God-given, is the cause of disvalue.

6 Process Theodicy and Free-Process Arguments

Process Theodicy

Process thought derives from the metaphysics of Alfred North Whitehead in *Process and Reality* (1929). In most of its theological variants it regards processes, at their most fundamental, as co-eternal with God. This gives rise to an alternative type of theodicy. God is neither responsible for the existence of what is not-God, nor is God able to prevent the inevitable conflicts between entities in their search for fulfilment. But God experiences and understands all the suffering that emerges in those conflicts. For a summary and evaluation of this form of theodicy, see Surin (1986: 86–92). For a classic exposition, see Cobb and Griffin (1976: Ch. 4). As they articulate process theodicy: 'the power of God is persuasive not controlling. Finite actualities can fail to conform to the divine aims for them' (70). And as these actualities grow in complexity, this 'makes greater enjoyment possible but also greater suffering' (72). There is a strong sense that evolutionary complexification is a good, leading to greater possibilities for intensity of experience. But 'God's stimulation of a more and more complex world, which has the capacity for more and more intrinsic value, means the development of creatures with more and more freedom to reject the divine aims.' (73–4) Contrary to almost all Christian formulations, process thought insists that the future is truly open – God's goodness is not necessarily victorious over evil. But Cobb and Griffin do offer a vision of the kingdom of heaven, based on God's everlasting receiving of the experience of creatures. I return to this move in Section 10.

This theodicy is successful in that its renunciation of divine power relieves the traditional tension between God's power and benevolence, but arguably it forfeits too many of the attributes of Christian theism (especially the ultimate victory of good) to be an effective contribution to our question. Process thought has however contributed some very important themes to the contemporary debate, including panpsychism (see Leidenhag 2020 for an exploration), divine lure (see Section 9 for the importance of this to an understanding of divine action), and divine co-suffering (also see Section 9).

Free-Process Arguments[21]

Free-process arguments regard God as having created natural processes and endowed them with freedom. These arguments regard freedom of process in nature as a good, which might outweigh the harms to which that freedom gives rise. They begin with the early theological responses to Darwinism, in which it was said, by for example, Charles Kingsley, that it was a good that God had made creation make itself (Brooke 1991: 293–4). The realisation that adaptation of creatures to their environment was a natural process, rather than a series of individual divine designs, enabled theologians to distance God from the detail of the unfolding of the process. God might then be distanced from direct responsibility for those adaptations (for instance, sabre-teeth in predators) that gave rise to creaturely suffering.

But that very phrase about making creation make itself reveals an ambiguity within free-process arguments that needs further investigation. Is the freedom of natural processes the good in itself, against which the harms that it causes may be balanced? This would be a property-consequence good-harm analysis (see Section 3). The alternative is that the freedom of process within the creation is a good because it allows values to develop, and hence furthers God's purposes in creation, making it possible for entities and systems to arise in a way more conducive to flourishing than if God had created them directly. The freedom would then be a developmental good.

---

[21] This section and the next section are reworkings of the argument of Southgate (2018b).

It is not clear to me that freedom of natural processes *is*, in the absence of divine goals, a 'good', certainly not a good that might balance myriad instances of creaturely suffering. Remember that the free-process argument is that natural processes are free, not simply that the living creatures that result from the operation of the processes have a degree of autonomy. The latter does seem to be an evident good. This autonomy of living creatures is enabled to *develop* through (a) God having given the creation laws that make the universe fruitful for life, and the world a consistent environment in which creatures can evolve effective strategies for flourishing, laws to which God remains faithful[22] and (b) God allowing some processes to which chance is intrinsic (such as mutation) to further the processes of evolution. But those seem to me developmental values, rather than goods in themselves.

The author of the phrase 'free-process defence' was the scientist-theologian John Polkinghorne. In *Science and Providence* (1989) Polkinghorne writes that:

> In his great act of creation I believe that God allows the physical world to be itself, not in Manichaean opposition to him, but in that independence which is Love's gift of freedom to the one beloved. The world is endowed in its fundamental constitution with an anthropic potentiality which makes it capable of fruitful evolution. (Polkinghorne 1989: 66)

Notably, Polkinghorne also allows for a very extensive divine providential interaction with the world. Such a position always intensifies the problem of theodicy. The more God involves Godself providentially in the flow of events, the more agonizing the issue of instances when God seems to do nothing. An extensive account of providence such as Polkinghorne's also complicates the assertion of freedom within natural processes. I discuss these questions of divine action further in Section 9.

In *Belief in God in an Age of Science* (1998) Polkinghorne explicitly admits that the free-process defence is a restatement of the nineteenth-century image of God making the world make itself (1998: 14). He takes this further in *Exploring Reality* (2005):

> creatures are allowed "to make themselves". This seems indeed to be a great good, but it also has a necessary cost. ... Things will often just *happen*, as a matter of fact, rather than for an individually identifiable purpose. (Polkinghorne 2005: 143, italics in original).

This last phrase might seem to suggest that Polkinghorne is adhering to freedom of creation as a non-instrumental, non-teleological good. In other words, that he

---

22 What Murray calls 'nomic regularity' (Murray 2008: Ch. 5).

regards the 'freedom' of entities – other than freely choosing conscious creatures such as humans – as still a good in itself. But I have always read him as
adhering to a more teleological view, albeit in respect of a generalised rather
than an 'individually identifiable' purpose. This is confirmed by his essay of
2012 in which he writes:

> The more science helps us to understand the world, the more clearly we see its
> inextricable entanglement of fertility and wastefulness. I have suggested that
> there is a Free-Process Defence in relation to natural evil, parallel to the
> familiar free-will defence in relation to moral evil. Natural evil is not gratuit-
> ous, something that a Creator who was a bit more competent or a bit less
> callous could easily have eliminated. Created nature is a package deal, with
> the emergence of new forms of life and the shadow side of malformation and
> extinction necessarily intertwined. (Polkinghorne 2012: 8–9)

Polkinghorne is not quite right about the parallel between the free-will and free-
process defences, since his understanding of the latter is really developmental,
to do with processes that lead to beneficial outcomes such as the emergence of
new forms of life, rather than the freedom of non-conscious entities being the
absolute good in itself, as in a property-consequence argument such as the free-
will defence. The freedom of natural processes, viewed instrumentally, in free-
process defences turns out not to be as closely analogous to the good of the
freedom of freely choosing rational agents to make those choices in free-will
defences as is sometimes supposed.

An important contemporary example of a free-process argument that is
authentically aligned with the form of free-will defences is that of Ruth Page
in *God and the Web of Creation*. Page writes:

> I cannot imagine a God responsible for natural evil any more than one
> responsible for moral evil ... To those who wish to affirm full-blooded ...
> [divine] making and doing, [my] version will appear anaemic. But the
> consequences of belief in a more virile God, who has to be responsible for
> the removal of around 98 per cent of all species ever, but who fails to do
> anything in millions of cases of acute suffering in nature and humanity, are
> scarcely to be borne. (Page 1996: 104)

Rather, Page wants to think of God as creating possibilities and then letting
them be – a very open form of making creation make itself, with a strong
cousinly resemblance to process thought. I am not clear that this altogether
relieves God of responsibility in respect of natural evil. After all, in this model,
God created, and continues to companion, particular possibilities, and therefore
still bears responsibility for their existence and for the suffering to which they
give rise.

What Page's formulation does address is what in Section 4 I called the teleological dimension of the problem of evolutionary disvalues – the thought that God used those disvalues to give rise to longer-term purposes. Page rigorously rejects this. God's purposes are confined to the creature itself, what she calls 'teleology now' (Page 1996: 63–73). She thus rejects the lure to complexification we noted above in process thought, though she formulates a moment-by-moment eschatology again very reminiscent of process schemes.

I conclude that Page's model must be regarded as a property-consequence free-process argument. It is the freedom of the creature that is the outweighing good that balances the suffering. As I implied above, there must be some question as to whether this is effective as a strategy in theodicy. First, because it does not 'get God off the hook', because God remains responsible for the existence of the processes that ultimately give rise to the disvalues. Second, because it is hard to accept this complete denial of longer-term teleology. Is God really agnostic as to whether divine companioning is of bacteria alone, or of single-celled organisms alone, or whether the divine desire for consciously given worship, so strongly attested in the Scriptures, points to a desire for a freely choosing self-conscious animal like the human? And with complexity, of course, comes an intensified capacity to suffer.

A further articulation of the free-process defence comes from Ryan McLaughlin in his *Preservation and Protest* (2014). He is very aware of the problem of theodicy in evolution, but like Page wants to find a way to draw back from assigning blame to God for the processes that give rise to suffering. He does this by an extraordinary move, claiming that God 'sets the world free *prior to the formation of its laws*' (McLaughlin 2014: 331).

This is, in effect, a further way of articulating the proposal of Page. There were primordial possibilities, and the creation 'chose' its own laws from within them. This is tricky both in relation to the shape of current cosmology, and to evolutionary theodicy. In the face of cosmological proposals that subvert the notion of an initial singularity, and suggest that the initial emergence of this universe might have been a random event, theologians are inclined to propose the reverse of McLaughlin, namely that it is through the underlying laws and parameters of the primordial state that God ensures the fruitfulness of the universe. This would indeed be a far more familiar understanding of the theology of creation.

But McLaughlin's proposal also faces the theological difficulty that I noted at the end of Section 5. It is the *same processes* that lead to disvalues in evolution that also give rise to all the values that we see. The laws that – for him – arose spontaneously within creation, and give rise to the disvalues we see in creation, *are the very ones* that make this creation the amazing phenomenon it is, and we have no evidence that a different set of laws would give rise to a more favourable balance between value and disvalue. I take up this issue in Section 7 on the only-way argument.

I end this section with a mention of Joshua Moritz's 'free creatures' defence, also published in 2014. Moritz is at pains to emphasise the new developments in evolutionary theory mentioned at the end of Section 4, and to downplay the role of natural selection in evolutionary outcomes. He is particularly struck by the theory of 'niche construction' – that creatures do not simply exist in an environment that is a given, but often shape that environment significantly. So creaturely behaviours are very significant in determining the character of ecosystems, and creatures may have options as to those behaviours and there-fore the niches they co-create. Thus far we are in agreement. I am however not at all convinced by Moritz's suggestion that the choices made by creatures are themselves the sole explanation for 'evil' in creation. There may be isolated instances in which a creaturely 'choice' directed a particular evolutionary trait down a particular path, but predation and parasitism are far too general phe-nomena, and (in the case of predation) far too generative of value (see e.g. Rolston 1992) for this type of explanation to be satisfactory.

I now turn to explanations that start from the premise that it is the same processes that generate both value and disvalue in the biosphere.

7 Only-Way Arguments

I have been one of the thinkers who have postulated what has come to be called the 'only-way' argument (e.g. Southgate 2008, 2018b). This is not by any means my invention, though the name is mine. It essentially goes like this:

'There is no reason to suppose that there was any way open to God by which God could have created a world with this richness of beauty, complexity, ingenuity and intricate interdependence of creatures with the opportunity to flourish, with a better balance between these values and the disvalues of struggle, competition, violence and suffering.'[23]

So yes, creaturely suffering is intrinsic to the world God has made, yes, it has been instrumental in realising God's purposes, but there was no better, less suffering-filled way available to God. Only-way theorists do not dissect out the world into the bits God willed and those that arose from distortions of that will. I argue that *scientifically* the world looks all of a piece, a 'package deal' in Niels Gregersen's phrase (Gregersen 2001),[24] and I also argue *theologically* that if

---

[23] This is, then, a scientifically nuanced version of Leibniz's Best of all Possible Worlds Argument.

[24] See also Ruse (2001); Fern (2002); Alexander (2008).

there had been a way to create a better balance of value against disvalue, a loving creator God would have adopted it.

The basic proposition behind the argument is that the disvalues in creation *necessarily arise* alongside the values. The disvalues may be understood as instrumental to the evolution of values, or as a by-product. Holmes Rolston stresses the instrumentality of the evolution process in the quotation already noted in Section 5 – 'the cougar's fang has carved the limbs of the fleet-footed deer, and vice versa' (Rolston 2006: 134). Nancey Murphy prefers to think of the suffering as a by-product (Murphy 2007). Either way, the two form a package deal. This indeed tends to be the reaction of biologists when questioned about the presence of predation and parasitism in nature.

The position is given philosophical attention by Robin Attfield. He concludes on rational grounds, without reference to Scripture or the doctrines of the Christian Church, that there might not be any 'better' created world that could be formulated for the realisation of creaturely value, and that that argument in itself constitutes a theodicy, even without recourse to other components such as an appeal to eschatology (Attfield 2006: 109–50). Another, more explicitly theological way to put this can be found in an essay of Arthur Peacocke's. He writes:

> If the Creator intended the arrival in the cosmos of complex, reproducing structures that could think and be free – that is, self-conscious, free persons – was there not some other, less costly and painful way of bringing this about? Was that the only possible way? This is one of those unanswerable metaphysical questions in theodicy to which our only response has to be based on our understanding of the biological parameters ... discerned by science to be operating in evolution. These indicate that there are inherent constraints on how even an omnipotent Creator could bring about the existence of a law-like creation that is to be a cosmos not a chaos, and thus an arena for the free action of self-conscious, reproducing complex entities and for the coming to be of the fecund variety of living organisms whose existence the Creator delights in. (Peacocke 2001: 36–7)

So although we are not in a position to be at all definite about this, it is a reasonable scientifically informed theological guess that a natural world containing creatures evolving by natural selection is the only way – or perhaps the best type of way – in which God could have given rise to the biological values we see within our own world. Indeed the 'Only-Way' argument receives support from a surprising quarter, from Richard Dawkins, arch-antagonist of theologians of evolution. Dawkins has written: 'if there is no other generalization that can be made about life all around the Universe, I am betting that it will always be recognizable as Darwinian life'. 'In short', 'if God was to create through law, then it had to be through Darwinian law. There was no other choice.' (Dawkins 1983: 423)

I have indicated that this is a type of argument favoured by a number of scholars coming from different approaches and traditions. I turn now to the objections that can be raised to it, and finally to what I consider to be its limitations.

The first objection might be posed by any student of the philosophy of religion. It is that the argument supposes a constraint on the supposedly omnipotent, omniscient Creator of the universe out of absolutely nothing. The objector is entitled to ask what the nature is of this constraint, and wherein it derives. To this the only-way theorist can only answer that the existence of the constraint is a plausible guess, and to advance a further guess that the constraint might be a logical one. In other words, it is a logical impossibility that a different mode of creation would have led to a world with a better balance of values to disvalues. We do not have access to this logic, but logical constraints are agreed to limit even an omnipotent God. Alternatively, there is a useful category in scholastic logic known as 'relative necessity' – given x, there must be y.[25] It is possible that, given the need to create physically embodied creatures in which could develop complexity, ingenuity of strategy, beauty, interdependence, and the capacity to flourish, the evolutionary process with its concomitant disvalues was a necessity. (This refinement of the only-way position is helpful to those subscribing to a belief in angels, since angels, in the tradition, are disembodied (or other-embodied) creatures possessed of beauty, intellect, and freedom of choice. God, seemingly, could create these de novo, but physically embodied creatures of the sort science describes seem only to arise out of an evolutionary process.)

Two extensions to the argument are pertinent at this point. First, the inference that it must have been impossible for God simply to create directly the eschatological state that Christians believe will follow from the ultimate redemption of the cosmos. God could not simply create heaven[26] (otherwise why did God not do so?) (Southgate 2008: 90; Russell 2019). I explore this further in Section 10. Second, that God may have been constrained as to the creation of worlds by God's loving desire that the world be redeemable through the incarnation of the divine Logos (Southgate 2014). We have no means of knowing if this further constrained the type of world that could have been created.

---

[25] Conti (2017). I am grateful to Dr Andrew Davison for pointing out this category of necessity.

[26] 'Heaven' is used throughout not as referring to a part of this physical universe but to that state of creatures in the new creation from which all struggle and suffering has disappeared, and in which God is 'all in all' (1 Cor. 15.28).

The second objection, raised by for example Neil Messer (2009), is that the only-way argument involves God being the creator of processes to which violence is intrinsic. For Messer this cannot be what is referred to in Genesis 1:31, when God calls creation 'very good'. This is a very important point, and only-way theorists must give an account of how their constrained creation is still 'very good'. That account could be based on the interpretation of that assessment of creation as 'good' as meaning 'that what has been made meets the [divine] intention' (Rogerson 1991: 61). The text from Deutero-Isaiah cited in Section 1, God the creator of 'weal and woe alike' (Is. 45.7), could also be adduced in support of this only-way creation. It must still trouble the only-way theorist that the ministry of Jesus – for Christians the greatest single clue to the character of God – seems to reject violence and be troubled by disease and death.

An objection to only-way thinking published by Mats Wahlberg warrants a careful analysis. Wahlberg's key point is that God, presumably knowing the precise molecular composition of the biosphere at any given moment, could create that molecular system *de novo*. So the result that God is presumed to desire could be obtained without the millennia of suffering necessitated by evolution (Wahlberg 2015). Two points may be made in response. The first is that of course that world would still be one full of predation and parasitism and driven by natural selection. So the problem of suffering in the non-human world would not be solved, merely mitigated. But the second point is more subtle. It is that living things, creaturely 'selves', are not merely a snapshot in time that could be photocopied by God. (The reader may consider whether God could reproduce an exact copy of the person she/he is at this instant of reading this section.) Creaturely selves have individual, and also ancestral, history. They have inherited experience that cannot altogether be reduced to molecular composition. So I am not persuaded of the reality of Wahlberg's thought-experiment.[27]

In 2008 Russell posed the question:

> Is this the best of all possible *universes* that God could have created with the intention of the evolution of life or could there be another kind of universe in which life evolved without natural evil? (Russell 2008: 255).

Russell could not be confident of this, which is why he focussed in that section on the redemptive dimension of evolutionary theodicy (see Section 10). This raises the question – why should God have to redeem, or heal, what God has created? How does the dynamic of redemption operate without a fall-event

---

[27] I thank Dr Bethany Sollereder for discussions on this point.

affecting the whole of creation? This is a very important and often-misunderstood element in this type of argument. To be wholly consistent, the narrative must run as follows:

There have been three great phases in God's action in the world. First, the creating, sustaining, and protecting from ultimate catastrophe of the 'old creation', which operates with the physical laws with which we are familiar, and the biological process of Darwinian evolution. Only such a process, productive alike of great value and huge amounts of struggle and suffering, could give rise to a world in which myriad types of physically embodied creature could flourish, and in which, as the second phase, the Logos could be incarnate and effect atoning transformation of an evolutionary world.

That atonement – however understood – makes possible the eschatological phase of God's work, the 'new creation' (Is. 65:17; 2. Cor. 5:17).[28] That phase leads ultimately to a dimension of existence in which there is no more suffering. But we are forced to conclude, if thinking this way, both that the initial ambiguous phase was a necessary preliminary, and also that the post-Cross eschatological phase is at a very early stage. The 'not yet' of Christian eschatology remains both an agony and a source of longing for the believer. Perhaps that enigmatic text, Romans 8:19–22, offers some insight into this – suggesting as it does that human redemption into authentic freedom is a necessary preliminary to final consummation (Southgate 2008: Chs. 6–7). Only then, so this model supposes, will come the final great action of God, the radical transformation of the physical universe, some laws retained and others, such as the second law of thermodynamics, suspended, such that (resurrected) bodily existence is possible without suffering or struggle. In this final state God is present to creatures in a yet more intense way, but without depriving them of individuality.

Note that the second phase is impossible without the first, and the third without the second. This in my view is the only way in which proponents of the only-way argument can resolve the tension we noted in Section 2, that the witness of Christ to the radically self-giving character of God seems at variance with an understanding of God as having created a world based on ruthless self-preservation.

The great strength of the only-way argument is that it recognises that the same processes give rise to great values and significant values, and accepts God's overall responsibility for both. But a shortcoming of the only-way argument is that it concentrates on the system as a whole. It suggests why an overall process – evolution by natural selection – might be essential to the development

---

[28] See Section 9 for further discussion of atonement.

of those values. But suffering is always particular to individual creatures. So for a more complete theodical response to the aporia of creaturely suffering, the only-way argument needs to be supplemented by a sense of God's co-suffering with creatures, an identification which reaches its climax at the Cross of Christ (Section 9), and by some vision of a redeemed existence for creatures in the new creation (Section 10).

8 Self-emptying and Cruciform Creation

We have seen one proposed constraint on the power of God that is intrinsic to the only-way argument, namely that a world evolving by natural selection, and therefore necessarily involving the suffering of sentient creatures, is the only sort of world in which the values represented by complex and diverse life could arise. Lloyd quite properly challenges only-way theorists to clarify the nature of the constraint on God (Lloyd 2018c: 329, see Section 12 for an attempt at this). A second constraint on God, amply familiar from Christian teaching, though still not univocally understood, is the necessity, oft-repeated in the New Testament, that Jesus should have to endure degrading execution to release, finally and fully, the redemptive purposes of God into the world.

The first of these constraints is unfamiliar to most Christians. The second is routinely confessed in various ways throughout the Church. But I would submit that they are comparable mysteries – indeed if anything the first is easier to understand than the second, since the first has the intuitions of the natural sciences to commend it, whereas the intuitions of a culture based on a sacrificial system are remote from us. Both carry that difficult sense that suffering might be instrumental to the divine purpose.

The fascinating move that Holmes Rolston makes is to fuse these two constraints, linking them via John 12.24: 'Unless a grain of wheat falls into the earth and dies, it remains alone, but if it dies, it bears much fruit.' He continues:

> Things perish with a passing over in which the sacrificed individual is delivered over to preserve a line. In the flesh and blood creatures, each is a blood sacrifice perishing that others may live. We have a kind of 'slaughter of the innocents', a nonmoral naturalistic harbinger of the slaughter of the innocents at the birth of the Christ, all perhaps vignettes hinting of the innocent lamb slain from the foundation of the world (Revelation 13.8). In their lives, beautiful, tragic, and perpetually incomplete, they have 'borne our griefs and carried our sorrows'. They share the labor of the divinity. (Rolston 2018: 748)

The typical answer to why Christ the Lamb is slain before the foundation of the world is that humans were bound to sin and be in need of blood-ransom. But

Rolston is implying a different answer, that sacrificial suffering is the necessary pattern by which life 'works'. He continues,

> Earth slays her children, a seeming evil, but bears an annual crop in their stead ... In a hurtless, painless world, there could never have come to pass anything like these dramas in botanical and zoological nature ... Death can be meaningfully integrated into the biological processes as a necessary counterpart to the advancing of life ... to be chosen by God is not to be protected from suffering ... The divine son takes up and is broken on a cross, 'a man of sorrows and acquainted with grief' (Is. 53.3) ... The capacity to suffer through to joy is a supreme emergent and an essence of Christianity. Yet, the whole evolutionary upslope is a lesser calling of this kind, in which renewed life comes by blasting the old. (Rolston 2018: 749)

Sallie McFague takes up this view of Rolston's in a recent essay (McFague 2020). She uses Rolston's contribution to the important collection of essays *The Work of Love: Creation as Kenosis*.[29] Rolston writes there: 'the picture coming more and more into focus has a great deal of one kind of thing being sacrificed for the good of another. The lives of individuals are discharged into, flow into, are "emptied into" these larger currents of life.' (Rolston 2001: 56).

McFague develops this through a Christological sketch centred on Phil. 2.5–8 'where the central movement is the self-emptying of God, becoming incarnate in a humble human being whose eventual end is death on a cross.' She continues: 'because Christians see God in the life, teachings and death of Jesus, kenosis or self-sacrificing is not just the story of Jesus but the story (interpretation) of God' (McFague 2020: 517). Therefore for McFague, 'a kenotic theology ... is a total interpretation, a new and different way of being in and understanding the world ... a model of sacrificial love for the neighbour is not only "good" for the other but close to "reality" as understood by evolutionary theory and some interpretations of the Christian understanding of God' (518). At once we may sense a problem. Creaturely suffering in evolution is largely not 'self-sacrificing' – animals typically do not choose their suffering.

In answer to the question, why is the life drama so suffering-filled, Rolston answers, in effect, that is the pattern of created reality, both of the evolutionary narrative and of God's ways with the world. The pattern has a kenotic hue to it. Moritz too offers this as the first of his proposals for mitigating the problem of evolutionary theodicy – the way of suffering is the way the God of Israel often works (Moritz 2014: 354). This formulation seems to beg, more than answer,

---

[29] 'Kenosis' is a theological term for self-emptying, especially of a sacrificial kind, deriving from the verb for Jesus' self-emptying at Phil. 2.7.

questions of theodicy, since God seems to impose the suffering of creatures as God's chosen pattern.

But McFague hints at a deeper insight. If Jesus in his kenotic self-emptying is the image of the invisible God (combining Phil. 2.7 with Col. 1.15), that invites us to develop a theology in which kenosis is intrinsic to the inner, Trinitarian life of God in Godself. So now the 'cruciform' pattern Rolston infers from both the natural world and the Christian story is not just a pattern stamped on created reality, but the pattern of divine life itself. This is an inference most developed in the thought of Hans Urs van Balthasar (though derived in turn from the speculations of Sergei Bulgakov). As Sarah Coakley explains,

> For Balthasar … the idea of kenotic self-surrender is too pervasive and important a characteristic of divine love to circumscribe its significance in christology alone; it is eternally true of the perichoretic and reciprocal interrelations of the persons of the Trinity, not something newly impressed on the divine by the events of the incarnation. (Coakley 2001: 199, cf. von Balthasar 1994: 323–4)

A thorough evaluation of this 'deep intratrinitarian kenosis' (so Southgate 2008: 58) is beyond the scope of this volume. It is enough here to guide the reader into this area. It is also important to articulate criticisms that could be levelled at this Rolston-McFague-Balthasar axis.

First, Rolston (and by extension McFague) may be criticised for presenting a 'resurrection-lite' faith. Rolston emphasises regeneration rather than resurrection (cf. 2018: 748). And it is striking that McFague ends her engagement with Phil. 2 at v.8, ignoring the hymn's triumphant conclusion that at the name of (the risen) Jesus 'every knee should bend' (Phil. 2.10) and every tongue confess his lordship. There seems little acknowledgement in Rolston, or in the essay of McFague's quoted here, of a future-transformed state of creaturely life with God (see Section 10).

Second, there is a criticism of von Balthasar's 'ur-kenosis' tellingly levelled by Karen Kilby. In important collections of essays on suffering and the Christian life, (Kilby 2020; Kilby and Davies 2020), which seek to avoid the neat systems that too many theodicies have attempted, Kilby argues that suffering and loss are not intrinsic to the life of the Trinity, or to the character of love. The Father's gift to the Son has no element of risk, emptying, or loss. Christ only suffered once, and though he was clearly not emotionally indifferent to his sufferings, there was, Kilby claims, an ultimate indifference – Christ's actions are taken as if there were no suffering and loss attached, as though the forces of death and destruction had no real existence. She calls this a kind of enacted *privatio boni*; suffering and loss are accorded no weight or influence.

She contrasts this with von Balthasar's insistence that we learn of the Trinity from the Cross, that there is within the Trinity an incomprehensible distance that in the economy of salvation becomes alienation and abandonment. Love and suffering are mutually internal to one another. For Kilby this effort to make sense of the world through a kind of integrated vision pays too high a price, and jeopardises the claim that the Gospel can really be good news.[30]

In this section we have seen that a possible way to account for the necessity of tragic suffering in evolution is to regard the suffering of creatures as essentially kenotic, and to trace that kenosis back into the life of God. God's creation, at least in respect of living things, would therefore be construed as in a sense in the divine image. This tempting move does still suffer from the critiques levelled by Kilby against deep intratrinitarian kenosis. I suggest however that this is a theodical fault-line where scientific evidence can weight the argument in one direction more than another. The massive extent of evolutionary suffering over deep time has led Rolston to characterise the long evolutionary history of the natural world, with creaturely suffering and sacrifice threaded through it, as 'cruciform' (Rolston 2006: 144). And if this is the character of creation as science now reveals it to us, that, arguably, adds weight to formulations of the Christian narrative as having an inescapably tragic dimension at its core.

Schneider at one point criticises Nancey Murphy for invoking kenosis for loss of self that is not freely chosen. If this was 'the only way of world making open to God' then this is not so much kenosis as 'the outworking of a tragedy, in which God is caught, as it were, as the central character of the play' (Schneider 2020: 124). Schneider himself takes a different line. He rejects the notion of a constraint on God. Rather God as supreme creative Artist chooses to operate in a particular way. Schneider reinterprets kenosis as God imposing suffering on individuals or groups. He reads this in Job, plausibly enough. Much more controversially he reads it in Christ's Passion, pointing to the prayer in Gethsemane as evidence that God worked in part against Christ's will. He writes,

> I suppose that this apparently needless and cruel enlistment of Jesus into such horrendous evil is what made the moral supremacy of Jesus' "kenotic" obedience possible ... I do not see how this treatment of the "Lamb of God" differs markedly in its moral substance from the alleged employment of animals as instrumental means to creative and redemptive ends (Schneider 2020: 207–8).

Schneider then links Rom. 8.20, God's subjection of creation to futility in hope, to Rom. 11.32 'For God has imprisoned all in disobedience so that he may be

---

[30] A more developed version of this argument will appear in Southgate (2023b).

merciful to all', regarding the rejection of the chosen people of God as a further example of this 'artistry' at work.

One thing I particularly admire in Schneider's book is his unflinching willingness to see God as 'the primary causal agent' responsible for evolutionary evils (2020: 43). But what he offers us as the cosmic artistry of the Creator, under the heading of kenosis, seems a disturbing travesty of these terms. The whole force of Phil. 2.7–8 is that Christ's kenotic self-emptying, whether that is understood in terms of his incarnation, his ministry, or his passion, is to be understood as the freest of choices. Even in Gethsemane Jesus' healthy human preference for life is freely sacrificed to the will of the Father. And I see the human choice of 'unbelief' (Rom. 11.20) as informing the treatment of Israel in Rom. 9–11. So I cannot see the analogy Schneider wants to draw between these human cases and that of non-human animals, who do not choose their suffering. He is right to challenge over-cosy descriptions of the sovereign God of the cosmos, but presses his case too far when he frames God's artistry in such high-handed terms, and adduces the category of creaturely kenosis as a God-driven process.[31] Nor is it clear exactly what greater outcome Schneider sees as made possible by the God-imposed 'kenosis' of non-human creatures.

Both the Rolston-McFague view and the Schneider view, then, break down on the disanalogy between creaturely disvalues and either 'sacrifice' or 'kenosis'. This in my view leaves the only-way argument, with all its limitations, as the best available account of the origin of evolutionary evils.

9 Questions of Providence and Divine Co-suffering

A neglected element of the question we are exploring is God's ongoing involvement with creatures across evolutionary history. Can we understand God as providentially involved in the lives of non-human creatures over evolutionary time, including those subject to predation and parasitism? What is God's providential relation to species extinction?

For a general overview of the issue of divine providence in Christian theology, see Fergusson (2018). For an important collection of essays on divine action in relation to evolution, see Russell et al. (1998). However, a prior question arises. A charge that an atheist might level at a monotheist in respect of biological evolution is this:

Given the apparently radical contingency of the process, riddled as it seems to be with chance events, and including as it has five major extinction events, and given that Darwinism, formally, does not admit of any directionality to the evolutionary process, is that process an appropriate one for an omnibenevolent

---

[31] On this he seems to commit the same error for which he had criticised Murphy.

deity to have used to give rise to a biosphere of creatures, evincing beauty, complexity, ingenuity of strategy, and interdependence?

The great extinction events, which each eliminated significant percentages of all species on earth, seem to argue for radical contingency and against a God-designed process. On the other hand, the only evolutionary history we know of has resulted in an overall rise in complexity and intricacy of interdependence, including the arising of an extraordinary species that knows (at least some of) the story of this history. Two important palaeobiologists have taken radically different views of this. Stephen Jay Gould asserts that:

> The diversity of possible itineraries [of evolution] does demonstrate that eventual results cannot be predicted at the outset. Each step proceeds for a cause, but no finale can be specified at the start, and none would ever occur a second time in the same way, because any pathway proceeds through thousands of improbable stages. Alter any early event, ever so slightly and without apparent importance at the time, and evolution cascades into a radically different channel. (Gould 1989: 51)

This leads to Gould's memorable conclusion that were the tape of evolution to run again, it would almost certainly lead to a completely different outcome. On this radically contingent view, the theist would have to conclude either that God had created a profoundly unreliable, as well as suffering-filled, process, or that God directed the process at every stage to give rise to outcomes God desired, including the evolution of human beings. (And as we noted in Section 6, such directing of the evolutionary process would intensify the theodical problem posed by suffering God seems to do nothing to address.)

On the other hand, Simon Conway Morris has insisted that certain types of outcomes were extraordinarily likely to emerge in evolution, sophisticated cognition being one of them (Conway Morris 2003). Conway Morris's key evidence comes from the phenomenon of convergence in evolution, whereby certain properties have arisen many times in separate evolutionary pathways. So a form of photosynthesis known as carbon-4 has emerged sixty-five times (Conway Morris 2022: 50). This view of evolution suggests that only a small proportion of the possibilities Gould talks of are actually explored in the 'tape', and that that proportion clusters around certain types of property that have proved extraordinarily useful to organisms (such as the camera eye). The theist might conclude from this that evolution is a plausible process by which God might reliably have given rise to certain sorts of creatures.[32] Such a model of

---

[32] Indeed Rope Kojonen goes as far as to suggest that the metaphor of divine design, which came under huge criticism after Darwin, might still be revived (Kojonen 2021).

theistic creation might not require any 'special divine action' by which God adjusted the course of evolution.

In an important article in 2018 Andrew Davison notes that:

> With further study since Gould's death, convergence has been more and more solidly confirmed. Significantly for our purposes, much of what turns out most clearly to have been converged also bears the greatest theological significance. The color of human skin or eyes and the number of digits on our fingers may well land with contingency and go to Gould. On the other hand, the story of evolution on earth shows multiple, independent evolutions of perception, intelligence, community, communication, cooperation, altruism, and construction. (Davison 2018: 1096–7)

So perhaps the possibility space of evolutionary outcomes is severely constrained in a way that makes the process look more like the product of divine design. Hoggard Creegan writes:

> What matters to theology here is that the process is not at heart one of randomness, driven only by the ever pressing will to survive and dominate others. There are deeper, more loving, gentler aspects at work that can be seen to set the direction of the evolutionary process (Hoggard Creegan 2013: 126).

There remains the question of those junctures when the whole project, or key parts of it, were profoundly threatened. Would God have stood by and allowed the whole of life on earth to go extinct? Would God have prevented the extinction of the line of *Homo Sapiens* when it faced a population bottleneck some 70,000 years ago?

These are fascinating theological puzzles. They are related to two other key questions, likewise unanswerable. First, what was God's role in the asteroid impact that led to the extinction of the dinosaurs and the rise of the mammals? Interestingly, Conway Morris in his most recent work suggests that mammals would have come to predominate anyway (2022: 84–94). Second and most pressingly, would God permit *Homo Sapiens* to exterminate themselves, either through nuclear catastrophe, or global pandemic, or runaway climate change? The theme of God only creating possibilities, and companioning them, is important in the model of Ruth Page, explored in Section 6. On God *protecting* possibilities as a cosmological as well as an evolutionary model, see Southgate (2011b: 300–3) and Section 12.

Robert J. Russell has proposed that God might have steered the course of evolution by using single, 'point' mutations in genomes as part of his model of non-interventionist objective divine action (Russell 1998). This is part of his sense that the flexibility of physical process at the quantum level allows God to influence the course of events with violating physical laws. It is not clear what extent of influence these non-interventionist interventions would be able to effect. For a critique of this type of approach to divine action, see Ritchie (2019). Russell's essay is representative of a quest for understandings of God's action that focussed on *mechanism*. But an arguably more important question concerns *morality*.

Consider the classic case of Rowe's fawn in the fire, outlined in Chapter 3. Do we see God altering that situation to prevent or reduce suffering? The argument of Clayton and Knapp in respect of other forms of natural evil is relevant here. They ask whether God could intervene occasionally (e.g. to prevent the cata-strophic tsunami of December 2004, or to minimise the loss of life by providing some at least with a warning of impending catastrophe) and conclude that even one such action would place on God the moral responsibility to intervene on every occasion when creaturely well-being was threatened. This is Clayton and Knapp's 'Not Even Once' precept (Clayton and Knapp 2011: Ch. 3). Indeed we do not seem to see non-human creatures rescued from their predicaments, though there must always be a caution about our applying our own (creaturely) morality to the creator of all.

This question of God's ongoing relationship to non-human creatures has received too little attention in the literature on evolutionary theodicy. So Sollereder's analysis (2019: Ch. 5) is particularly important. She includes divine co-presence with the creature, divine lure to the creature to act for its own selving, the incarnation of the Christ understood as God's joining cre-ation by taking flesh as creature, and God as shaper of the meaning of events (a theme she develops in her treatment of life after death for creatures, see Section 10 of the present volume). She also takes issue with Clayton and Knapp's proposals. They contend that although the physical sciences offer a complete description of how events operate at the physical level, God can interact with creatures at the mental level, because mental events are not reducible to physical brain events. This view can be challenged, as after all what are brains made of but physical matter? But also, for Sollereder, the Clayton-Knapp proposal allows too little scope for God to act, especially given God's great action in the Incarnation.

The motif of divine lure, however, attracts Clayton and Knapp, Sollereder, and also myself (Southgate 2008: Ch. 4). It derives in the first instance from process thought (see Section 6). Out of love, the process God lures creatures towards harmony and fulfilment. Sollereder however points out that creatures being truly themselves does not necessarily imply harmony – they may be predators, or parasites, and their flourishing therefore requires violence towards other creatures. Sollereder is clear that this is the character of the creation. She is also attracted to my own proposal that the divine lure includes an invitation to self-transcendence, to the exploration of novel behaviours (Sollereder 2019: 140, cf. Southgate 2008: 61–3).

Divine Co-suffering

A common motif in a range of evolutionary theodicists is God's co-suffering with suffering creatures (for Sollereder an aspect of God's co-presence, 2019: 135–7). This raises two important questions. First, is it meaningful to speak of God suffering? Second, what difference might it make to a suffering creature that God co-suffers with it?

To tackle this first question, I note how theologians steeped in the traditional position that God cannot suffer may nevertheless nuance their views in helpful ways. So Denis Edwards explains that holding to divine impassibility 'rules out fickleness, arbitrariness, and inconstancy, and all the emotions and passions unworthy of God'. But he continues, 'It does not rule out God-befitting emotions, such as love, compassion and generosity ... of Godlike kind, infinitely beyond all human emotions' (Edwards 2018: 685). Hans Urs von Balthasar too wants to hold formally to impassibility but says that 'There is something in God that can develop into suffering' (1994: 328). While noting the point that insofar as God might suffer, God can neither experience ungodlike emotions, nor be destroyed, rendered not-God, by suffering (although the identity of humans can be so destroyed), many theologians want to insist on the meaningfulness of divine co-suffering. For McDaniel as a process theologian this is intrinsic to the character of God 'as Heart' (McDaniel 1989). For Peacocke it is an outworking of his emphasis on divine indwelling. He writes:

> God suffers in and with the sufferings of created humanity and so, by a natural extension, with those of all creation, since humanity is an evolved part of it. The suffering of God, which we could glimpse only tentatively in the processes of creation, is in Jesus the Christ concentrated to a point of intensity and transparency which reveals itself to all who focus on him. (Peacocke 1998: 372)

Fascinatingly, a slightly later essay alters this to '..intensity and transparency that reveals it as expressive of the perennial relation of God to the creation' (Peacocke 2001: 42). This begins to explore the vital theological question – what is the relation between the unquestionable suffering of the divine Son at the Cross, and the co-presence of God with all living creatures over evolutionary time? Is the Cross the sole locus of divine suffering, or its particular focus, or illustrative of its generality?

A careful analysis of the arguments for and against divine impassibility can be found in Fiddes (2000: Ch. 5). Fiddes looks at the basis of a range of claims of impassibility, grounded in Scripture, tradition, reason and experience, and nevertheless concludes that:

> God is always entering with sympathy into the lives of creatures. It is not only in the particular point in history of the cross of Jesus Christ that God makes a journey into human life and is changed by the experience. (186)

And if into human life, then surely also into the lives of all creatures that suffer. But we may still ask: what *difference* does the divine suffering co-presence make to suffering creatures? I offer the suggestion: 'that God's suffering presence is just that, presence, of the most profoundly attentive and loving sort, a solidarity which at some deep level takes away the aloneness of the suffering creature's experience' (Southgate 2008: 52, see also 2014).

Another dimension of this question is the refrain in the Psalms that all creatures praise God (e.g. Ps. 19.1–6). In a remarkable passage Karl Barth suggests that perhaps creation praises God most intensely in what he called its 'shadowy side'. He writes:

> creation and creature are good even in the fact that all that is exists in this contrast and antithesis ... For all we can tell, may not His creatures praise Him more mightily in humiliation than in exaltation, in need than in plenty, in fear than in joy, on the frontier of nothingness than when wholly orientated on God (Barth 1961: 296–7)

For Barth, not only may we postulate that God is a companion in the creature's suffering, but that the creator-creature relationship is actually intensified in suffering. The creature's dependence on, pre-conscious awareness of, the source of its life, and the response of praise, is if Barth is right at its most intense in times of suffering. And God's commitment to being present to the creature, which is always there, may perhaps develop a new intensity in these times (cf. Southgate 2018a: 133–4).

Incarnation and Atonement

Sollereder is surely right to see the Incarnation of Christ, however understood, as a central element in divine action, and to see the divine Word taking flesh (Jn. 1.14) as God's identification not just with humanity but with all life. More than that, Christian thought-frameworks see the Christ-event as transformative, and inaugurating a phase of redemption leading ultimately to the consummation of all things. That atoning work of Christ is confessed at Col. 1.20 as being cosmic in scope. It is not easy to see how to apply theories of atonement to the non-human creation, especially if it is acknowledged as unfallen (Sollereder 2019: Ch. 2). Three thoughts may be helpful:

(a) that in being incarnate as flesh, and taking the form of a suffering servant, God in Christ takes responsibility for the suffering throughout creation. So for Frances Young, 'God needs to make reparation for creating a world like this, otherwise there can be no atonement' (2013: 247).

(b) that God in Christ inaugurates a new freedom of life in the Spirit for humans, and that this is for whatever reason a necessary preliminary to the full birthing of the new creation (cf. Rom. 8.19–22).

(c) that if there is even an element of angelic or spiritual resistance to God affecting the non-human world (see Sections 5 and 13) Christ's victory over those powers might be a necessary preliminary to eschatological transformation.

This section on divine action offers more questions than answers, testament to the difficulty of the issue. I advance a further, very speculative account in Section 12. Whether divine involvement with the experience of suffering creatures is framed in Edwards's terms, or in Sollereder's, or McDaniel's, that intimate involvement forms a component in the theological puzzle we are exploring. It often sits alongside a free-process or only-way argument (Sections 6 and 7), but it is also often found alongside a claim that some or all suffering creatures will have some sort of immortality beyond death, and this we go on to explore in Section 10.

10 Forms of Redemption and Immortality for Non-human Creatures

Compared with the very strong and repeated affirmations of resurrection for human beings, there is very little in the Christian tradition about post-mortem existence for non-human creatures. Nevertheless there are scriptural and theological reasons for postulating such existence, as follows:

Scripturally, a few texts point in this direction. In Isaiah we see visions of what is sometimes called the 'peaceable kingdom' in which domesticated animals co-exist in peace with their natural predators (Is. 11.6–9; 65.25). Certain texts in the New Testament seem to imply a 'cosmic' reach to divine redemption, such as Rom. 8.19–22, Col. 1.15–20, and Eph. 1.10. But this is fragmentary evidence.

Theologically, one could argue that the resurrection life of humans would be impoverished if it were lived without community with other animals. But also the argument can be made that theodicy requires post-mortem existence for animals. This proposal goes back at least to a famous sermon of John Wesley's, preached almost eighty years before the publication of *The Origin of Species*. Wesley opined that there might be:

'a plausible objection against the justice of God, in suffering numberless creatures that had never sinned to be so severely punished ... But, the objection vanishes away, if we consider, that something better remains after death for these creatures also; that these likewise shall one day be delivered from this bondage of corruption, and shall then receive an ample amends for all their present sufferings.' (Wesley 1825: 131)[33]

This section will consider the possible nature of this post-mortem existence, and what would constitute 'amends' for sufferings in this life. Several of our major sources devote space to this question, such as Murray 2008: 122–9; Southgate 2008: Ch. 5; Sollereder 2019: Ch. 6, and there are important theories proffered by Dougherty (2014) and Schneider (2020). I also note that Russell concludes that evolutionary theodicy must be based on the redemption of creatures, since other theodicies fail to deliver (2008: Ch. 8). Moltmann also argues that:

A *Christus evolutor* without *Christus redemptor* is nothing other than a cruel, unfeeling *Christus selector*, a historical world-judge without compassion for the weak, and a breeder of life uninterested in the victims ... Not even the best of all possible stages of evolution justifies acquiescence in evolution's victims ... There is therefore no meaningful hope for the future of creation unless 'the tears are wiped from every eye'. But they can only be wiped away when the dead are raised, and when the victims of evolution experience justice through the resurrection of nature. Evolution in its ambiguity has no such redemptive efficacy and therefore no salvific significance either. If Christ is to be thought of in conjunction with evolution, he must become evolution's redeemer. (Moltmann 1990: 296–7)

So, again, a theory of creaturely immortality must consider what 'justice' would require. A key distinction within theories of immortality is between *objective and subjective immortality*. In theories of objective immortality the experience of the creature, or all that is positive in that experience, is retained everlastingly in the memory of God. This is a characteristic move in process thought, and is also embraced by John Haught, who writes: 'the whole story of the universe and life streams into the everlasting bosom of divine compassion' (Haught 2005: 17). Or to put it another way, 'Somehow every event in cosmic process is salvaged and preserved eternally in God in full immortality (Haught 2004: 157–8). So also Jay McDaniel: 'the grey whale and the orca are brought together in God's experience ... and they are, in this way 'redeemed'' (McDaniel 1998: 169).

This is the easiest type of theory to hold, requiring as it does no great flight of imagination about creatures, only a very plausible presumption about the

---

[33] Note that this runs counter to much of the Christian tradition, exemplified by Aquinas denying non-human creatures immortal souls (Murray 2008: 123).

everlasting and all-encompassing memory of God. So it is striking how many theodicists want to say more, to embrace some form of *subjective immortality*, in which the creature has some form of embodied post-mortem experience, in their own identity though without suffering. That is in tune with the scriptural and theological hints we noted above, but it raises all sorts of questions. Is every creature resurrected, or only those with sufficient sentience to have meaningful experience of resurrection life? How can predators who have lived by hunting and killing be themselves in this resurrection life? What constitutes 'amends' or 'justice' for creatures which have experienced no fulfilment in their first lives? And lastly but importantly, if this suffering-free existence is possible, why did God not simply just create this 'heaven'?

Sollereder has the most comprehensive analysis of these questions. She deploys McDaniel's analysis of redemption as having four aspects: 'freedom from the consequences of sin ... ; freedom from what distresses or harms ... ; contribution to lives beyond one's own ... ; transformation into an improved state of existence' (Sollereder 2019: 156–7, based on McDaniel 1989: 42). The first she discards, since in her view the category of sin is reserved for humans.[34] The third she identifies with the views of Holmes Rolston, who has written eloquently about the way in which a creature's death feeds their body into a food-chain of other lives (Rolston 1994; see our discussion in Section 8). As to the other two, all scenarios of post-mortem existence presume a freedom from what distresses or harms, which is part of the 'improved' character of that existence.

For McDaniel the problem is not death but incompleteness (1998: 170). So a period of post-mortem fulfilment need not be everlasting. For Denis Edwards, the form of immortality will be that appropriate to the creature (Edwards 2006). For some that might be a subjective immortality, for others, being held within the life of the Triune God. Whereas for Moltmann and Sollereder resurrection is universal, a mind-boggling notion given the myriad life-forms that have existed, but given that 'heaven' is taken to be characterised by a lack of the constraints that inform life in this age, there need not be any shortage of space.

Two factors are in tension in the imagining of subjective immortality. The first is *continuity of identity* – that resurrected leopards retain their leopardness. That would tend to imply that there might still be hunting of prey, even if without distress or harm. I have explored this idea (Southgate 2008: 88–9), and it is skilfully modified by Sollereder when she suggests that the experience, for both resurrected predator and resurrected prey, would be akin to sporting

---

[34] Whereas David Clough, for example, has wanted to extend notions of sin to other animals (Clough 2012: Ch. 5), which takes us back in the direction of Moritz's 'free creatures defence' discussed in Section 6.

contests (2019: 167). But the more the resurrected life is aligned with the mortal life, the weaker the sense of amends or justice. Is mere continuity of experience beyond death, admittedly suffering-free, compensation for whatever experience of distress and harms the first life contained? As Dougherty puts it: 'Reparations, even if they are in some way sufficient for damage done, do not buy one's way out of the guilt of one's actions' (2014: 98). It may be held that God's responsibility for creaturely suffering is not cancelled by merely compensatory resurrection.

So the other factor is *transformation*. Both Dougherty (2014) and Schneider (2020) suppose that the resurrected state of creatures will include enhanced cognitive awareness, though the approaches taken are different. For Dougherty, the most plausible theodicy is an 'Irenaean' theodicy of the type developed by Hick (1966), in which suffering allows 'soul-making', which Dougherty extends to the development of the sorts of virtues that are characteristic of saints – faith, hope, and love, especially self-transcending love. It is very difficult to apply that to non-human animals, but Dougherty seeks to do so (2014: Chs. 8–9).

For Dougherty animals' capacity to make meaning out of their lives is, yes, very limited in this life, but then so is that of human infants. If a human dies in infancy, we presume that God will make possible soul-making beyond death, and Dougherty suggests that can also be true for animals. In fact both humans and animals need post-mortem enhancement of their cognitive capacities in order fully to understand their lives. In both cases, the creature will ultimately be able to accept the suffering they experienced 'as an integral part of a very good life' (2014: 150).

Schneider is not convinced that this purgatorial process of meaning-making is needed. He also questions whether Dougherty has not strayed too far from the continuity of identity mentioned above. Schneider prefers a view in which, in the transformed conditions of the new creation, animals who have played their part in their evolutionary process are celebrated as 'martyrs', who receive 'universal admiration, gratitude, and praise from God, the angels and humans for what they have done' (2020: 268). They do not, on this view, need to understand the 'why' behind what they may have suffered, just to receive the celestial praise.

The most sophisticated model is provided by Sollereder with her 'fractal mosaic model of redemption' (2019: 165–73). This complex proposal should be read in the original, but here are some key points. Every creaturely life is like a tile of a mosaic, or, better, a tile inscribed with a video of that life. The centre of the mosaic is the Incarnate Christ, the '"organising algorithm" of redemption' (177). 'The creatures that once suffered are drawn into the work of the cross, and aligned with all other creatures into a dynamic mosaic of praise. All hurts are healed, all relationships mended, and all creatures . . . live out the praise of God' (177). God, then, is dynamically at work organising the mosaic of creaturely lives into patterns of meaning, and this includes the fullness of life experienced by creatures after death.

It remains to consider why God did not just create a cosmos free of suffering and struggle in the first place. I tackle this question in *The Groaning of Creation* by means of an extension of the only-way argument. I write:

> Since this was the world the God of all creativity and all compassion chose for the creation of creatures, we must presume that this was the only type of world that would do for that process. In other words, our guess must be that though heaven can eternally preserve those selves, subsisting in suffering-free relationship, it could not give rise to them in the first place. (Southgate 2008: 90)

Robert Russell has reflected further on this claim, as follows:

> I will refer to this as the "heaven requires earth" argument . . . I believe it is an essential, and not just an ancillary, argument to Southgate's overall theodicy for several reasons . . . It offers an intricate and important new element that should be added to the existing six elements of Southgate's "only way argument." . . . Without it, Southgate's theodicy could easily fall prey to a dualistic ontology of creation in which a radical, gnostic split would forever exist between our material universe ("creation"), with the scientific predictions of an eternal future of endless expansion, lifelessness, and dissolution, and "heaven" ("new creation") as an ontologically separate and strictly spiritual abode immunized forever from the history of life in our universe, including the Gospel of Christ. Instead, with this new element, Southgate's theodicy insists that "heaven and earth" are held together as the domain of God's creating and redeeming Spirit in which "all will be well." . . . "Heaven requires earth" is, as best I know, an almost unique insight in the field of natural theodicy, and in natural and moral theodicy as a whole. It's (sic) extraordinarily profound yet utterly simple claim is, to me at least, astonishing, liberating, and compelling. (Russell 2019: 192)

Mention of my compound theodicy takes us to an overall evaluation of the theological moves we've considered, and whether a combination of these moves forms the best way to shed further light on the deep puzzle we are considering.

11 Combining Strategies

It is striking how many thinkers writing in this area have wanted to combine theological moves to generate an overall theodicy. Working philosophically, Murray writes:

For all we know,[35] however, animal pain and suffering might be explained in part by each of the following:

(1) The good of a world in which there are nonhuman animals capable of good, spontaneous, and intentional actions.
(2) The good of preserving organismic integrity in a world where animals are liable to physical harm.
(3) The good of an eternal existence where animals can enjoy, in limited respects, the goodness of the presence of God.
(4) The good of a nomically regular world which supports free and effective choice, intellectual inquiry, and a good and diverse created order.
(5) The good of a universe which moves from chaos to order.

(Murray 2008: 196–7, section and chapter numbers omitted)

To clarify, Murray's (2) is about the positive value of pain in sentient organisms. Murray's (4) is about a world lawful and consistent enough for human rationality to develop and lead to real human freedom of choice.[36] He is clear that of itself this move is not adequate as a theodicy of *animal* suffering. It needs to be supplemented by his move (5), that animal suffering is an unavoidable developmental by-product of the process that, over vast reaches of time, gave rise to rationality and freedom, especially in the human though embryonically in other animals.[37]

When these arguments are combined, Murray can formulate his conclusion as follows: 'do we have any grounds for affirming that it *does not* explain why God permits so much animal pain and suffering rather than a lot less? I think the answer to this question is ... surely no' (2008: 198, italics in original).

Schneider raises the bar for theodicy by asking not only that 'one's account must at least be *as plausible as not* overall, but also provide 'a perspective in which to "see" divine power and goodness in the midst of the Darwinian evil unveiled and thereby help to restore "theistic sight"' (2020: 70, italics in original). His perspective combines the following:

First, Schneider mounts a theological comparison of the kenosis of Jesus, the God-imposed kenosis of Israel in Rom. 9–11, and what he sees as the God-imposed kenosis of those creatures who are the victims of evolution. This is God as 'Artist', as vine-dresser, seen 'through eyes of a certain sort of messianic faith' (217).[38] Therein lies the basis for Schneider's theistic seeing. But just as the evil

---

[35] A formulation that recalls van Inwagen in his Gifford Lecture (2006: Lecture 7).
[36] Clayton and Knapp, pursuing a similar line though not explicitly considering non-human suffering, add the importance of such a world making science possible (2011: Ch. 3).
[37] There is a link here to the only-way argument, and also to the nineteenth-century celebrations of God having made a universe that could make itself.
[38] I commented on this argument in Section 8.

of Jesus' passion would not be defeated except by his resurrection, so the evil of animal suffering requires that those creatures too experience resurrection (216), and not just resurrection but acclamation as martyrs (see Section 10).

Sollereder too wants to combine different moves in constructive theology, by providing answers to the three questions: 'How does God love? How does God act? How does God redeem?' (2019: 93). And as we saw in Sections 9 and 10, in discussing both divine action and divine redemption she combines multiple modes of understanding. Implicitly too she seems to embrace elements of only-way and free-process arguments.

In 2008 I provided perhaps the most explicit formulation of a 'compound theodicy'. I write:

☐ I acknowledge the pain, suffering, death and extinction that are intrinsic to a creation evolving according to Darwinian principles. Moreover, I hold to the (unprovable) assumption that an evolving creation was the only way in which God could give rise to the sort of beauty, diversity, sentience and sophistication of creatures that the biosphere now contains. As shorthand I call this the 'only-way' argument.

☐ I affirm God's co-suffering with every sentient being in creation – the 'co-suffering' argument.

☐ I take the Cross of Christ to be the epitome of this divine compassion, the moment of God's taking ultimate responsibility for the pain of creation, and – with the Resurrection – to inaugurate the transformation of creation.

☐ I further stress the importance of giving some account of the eschatological fulfilment of creatures that have known no flourishing in this life. A God of loving relationship could never regard any creature as a mere evolutionary expedient. Drawing on a phrase of Jay McDaniel's, I nickname this the 'pelican heaven' argument.

☐ If divine fellowship with creatures such as ourselves is in any sense a goal of evolutionary creation, then I advocate a very high doctrine of humanity, supposing that indeed humans are of very particular concern to God. That does not in any way exclude a sense that God delights in every creature which emerges within evolution, but it leads to the possibility that humans have a crucial and positive role, co-operating with their God in the healing of the evolutionary process – the 'co-redeemer' argument.

(Southgate 2008: 16, section numbers deleted)

Reflecting on these approaches takes us back to the contrast between philosophical and theological strategies. Murray is compiling an argument that defends theism as at least as plausible as not. He is clear that concentrating on the eventual benefits to humans of a consistent world is not adequate, and has to include his developmental move (5).[39] Schneider requires of his theodicy not only plausibility but also theistic seeing – 'to look Darwinian evil fully in the face, to look more deeply into it than we have perhaps yet done, in so doing, seek to discern divinity directly in its midst' (2020: 45). He adopts different arguments for his two different requirements.

My term 'compound theodicy' might mislead the reader. It is best seen not as an argument in which different propositions combine to form a case for plausibility, but as an exploration of the ways in which reflection on suffering in evolution might affect the construction of a Christian theology which, while tentative and exploratory, might seem to hold together for a worshipping community. I sense that Sollereder is also attempting this.

I have now summarised what I see as the main elements in the contemporary debate about evolutionary theodicy. In the two last sections I offer some more speculative proposals which I hope will stimulate future explorations.

12 Speculative Proposal I – Influenced by Plato's *Timaeus*

In this first speculation I draw on Plato's enigmatic but enormously influential dialogue the *Timaeus*, which postulates a demiurge using intelligence (*nous*) to give rise to the tangible creation by working with imperfect materials. I am thereby able to offer a possible development of the only-way argument.[40]

Plato speaks of the 'receptacle' into which creation is 'cast', which is sometimes spoken of as resembling 'matter' and sometimes more as 'space'. This '*chōra*' has attracted the attention of Catherine Keller, in her important meditations on the 'tehom' of Gen. 1.2 (Keller 2003). Keller invokes two very different thinkers who also want to work with *chōra* – Alfred North Whitehead and Jacques Derrida (Keller 2003: 165–7). Virginia Burrus devotes the first part of her recent essay on ecopoetics to *chōra* (Burrus 2019). Clearly, the sense of a primordial 'stuff', with potential but without God-endowed form, continues to fascinate.

Plato also speaks of the necessity (*anangkē*) that is combined with reason in giving rise to the phenomenal universe as a *planōmenē aitia*, a wandering or errant cause. The combination of these three factors – *nous*, *anangkē*, and *chōra* – could be used to fashion an account remarkably similar to one of the ways in which a scientifically informed theology of creation might be framed.

In saying this I am not for a moment supposing that Plato had any sense of this. Indeed he is very properly criticised for preferring idealised schemata to those based on attention to actual phenomena. But if Simon Conway Morris is

---

[39] For completeness I should note that Murray regards a rebellion of the angels, considered by itself, as also a plausible defence of God (2008: 106).

[40] This proposal is found in more developed form in Southgate (2023a).

right that the landscape of evolutionary possibility contains certain 'attractors', such as the camera eye, and more importantly intelligence,[41] then it is possible to formulate a theological postulate that God designed this landscape such that certain creaturely properties were almost bound to arise, given time (and survival of catastrophic pan-extinctions). This design could be seen as the operation of *nous*, and the landscape could be understood as analogous to Plato's *chōra*, the 'filled space' of biological possibility. Crucially, the 'wandering cause' of natural selection of heritable variants (combined with such recent emphases in evolutionary theory as niche construction, epigenetic inheritance, etc.), supplies the third ingredient, the mechanism by which the space of possibility is traversed, and 'solutions' involving the fundamental attractors of convergent evolution are 'explored'. This is 'necessity', that kind of 'relative necessity' we noted in Section 7, given that there are to be physical creatures. But this necessity is governed by 'intelligence' in being shaped by certain attractors, so that the results of the wandering cause are not truly random but do manifest a tendency towards certain types of adaptiveness to environment.

I am very attracted to Page's proposal that what God creates, first of all, is a range of possibilities (Page 1996: 12–21). Suppose then that God gives rise first of all to a whole range of possibilities, to a 'possibility space' (analogous to a multidimensional fitness landscape in evolutionary theory). Think of these as the *chōra*, the 'receptacle' for all actual existents.[42] Only some, perhaps a very small proportion of these possibilities, can give rise to a life-bearing universe. That is a logical constraint, necessity constraining what even the divine reason can make happen. These possibilities give rise by processes involving a significant degree of randomness[43] to actual mass-energy-space-time universes. Many possible universes may decay instantly. But let us suppose that God *protects* one or a range of universes that have the potential to be life bearing.[44] God accompanies these universes as they develop under the influence both of the laws God has created and the randomness intrinsic to quantum processes. Additional possibilities then arise which God could foresee in general but not in particular.

The sciences still have no way of knowing how likely life was to arise even on a 'habitable' planet. But let us further say that God protects a range of possibilities

---

[41] See Section 9, also Davison (2018): 1089–94.

[42] The ancient metaphysicians would have understood 'matter' not as modern science would conceive it but as 'the substrate that makes form, or intelligibility, possible in a thing.' (Hincks 2018: 327).

[43] That there is any structure to the universe at all is sometimes attributed to (utterly random) quantum fluctuations in a suddenly inflating universe. See Greene 2004: 305–10.

[44] This model then exhibits two classic properties of *ex nihilo* theologies of creation: it calls God the reason why there is anything and not nothing, and also the reason why what contains form, meaning, and value does not decay to nothing.

that can give rise not just to systems that might meet the definition of being alive, but have the potential to develop further complexity. Again, the precise nature of that emerging complexity might not be known in advance by God, who continues to accompany possibilities and protect those that can give rise to certain types of value, such as beauty, complexity, diversity, and intelligence.

Vital to this theory, then, is the rationality of God-given laws, but also a 'receptacle' of possibility that is God's first creation, and a 'wandering cause', which involves both quantum indeterminacy and, once life has arisen, the processes of natural selection, genetic drift and niche construction that shape organisms and environments in an interdependent way. To these Platonic ingredients, however, are added an authentic sense of creation *ex nihilo*, and also a sense of God's personal providential care for creation as it unfolds, a care that accompanies, rather than determines, but which prevents the total destruction of generative possibilities. The model recognises that only a narrow range of possibilities can be life bearing, and a still narrower range can lead to complex life; also that these life-fruitful systems develop through physical and biological processes that necessarily lead to a blend of value and disvalue.

What I have attempted here is a speculative account (as Plato indeed regarded the *Timaeus*) that tries to put flesh on the idea that only via an evolutionary process could certain sorts of creaturely properties emerge. It does not demonstrate the truth of the only-way argument, which ultimately has to be argued for theologically by appeal to the goodness of God. But it fills in a little of the detail of how necessity might constrain the divine creative intent. In doing so it makes links with the thought of perhaps the greatest of all Western philosophical thinkers, while retaining the Christian confession that an infinitely transcendent, infinitely compassionate God is the reason for the existence of anything rather than nothing.

13 Speculative Proposal II – Creaturely Resistance and Angelic Rebellion

I offer here a second proposal, which draws on elements on Sections 5, 6, and 7. In an important book published in 1988 Paul Fiddes argued this: 'Some overall vision of the "responsiveness" and "resistance" of creation to the Spirit of God is needed for a doctrine of creative evolution, [and] for a proper theodicy' (Fiddes 1988: 228). I've long been intrigued by this sentence. What if anything resists the Spirit of God in the unfolding creation? A strict only-way theorist would say – nothing. God has put in place a system that has the best balance between values and disvalues. Both values and disvalues serve the purposes of God, who may not determine the character of the world in every detail, but specifies its overall behaviour. Non-human creatures just do what they do, however ugly it may sometimes seem to us.

No resistance to the divine invitation need be postulated. Not until we see human sin do we see resistance to God's will in creation.

But that instinct Fiddes draws on is strong. Also, the strict only-way argument can be criticised for making an artificially sharp divide between the human and our evolutionary past. Only with humans comes freedom to choose evil over good. That might be correct, but the evolutionary theorist will want to probe such a claim. When exactly in human evolution did such freedom arise? Has it no precursor in the non-human world? Celia Deane-Drummond claims that,

> tendencies towards sin are also in pre-human life. Just as agency is latent in the world prior to the emergence of full-blown human freedom, so, tendencies towards viciousness are present in animal communities even prior to the kind of deliberative cruelty that is such a distinctive characteristic of our kind (Deane-Drummond 2018: 799)

She is referring here for instance to accounts of violence among chimpanzees. David Clough too uses examples of primate infanticide and cannibalism to suggest there could be sin in non-human animals (Clough 2012: 112–19). So perhaps there is a hint of resistance here, though the only-way theorist cannot go as far as to agree with Joshua Moritz that creaturely choices are the sole source of evil in biology (Moritz 2014; see Section 6 for a critique). Nor can I agree with Clough that predation in itself necessarily manifests the sort of overplus of viciousness that might lead us to speak of resistance to the divine will. The tiger does not sin when it stalks the goat. It is simply following its evolved nature, which manifests great beauty, power, and skill.

So I have been pondering where we might see hints of resistance, within an overall picture of an evolving world that has led, despite great periods of extinction, to an extraordinary development of creaturely complexity, ingenuity, beauty, and interdependence. I wonder whether the phenomenon of parasitism might not have about it a hint of resistance to the divine Spirit. If we suppose that God's purposes in creation include the development of greater and greater creaturely complexity and interdependence, then an evolutionary strategy that feeds on complexity to promote a simpler entity might seem to smack of resistance. Parasitism may arise out of 'cheating' (in a game-theory sense) on an arrangement of biological mutualism (a subject on which Andrew Davison has written recently, Davison 2020a and 2020b); parasitism may therefore be thought of as a kind of parody of interdependence. A related argument could be framed in relation to cancers, which in a sense reverse evolution, feeding on the body's complexity to make quantities of simple tumour tissue. This seems to me to be a promising area in which to speak, however tentatively, of a certain element of resistance to the divine will.

The COVID pandemic that spread through the world in 2020 has focussed much attention on viruses. And what I've just said about parasites might be said all the more of viruses. Like parasites, they may exhibit great ingenuity of evolutionary strategy – to learn more of COVID-19 is to be more and more impressed by its mechanisms of operation. But viruses don't just manufacture simpler life at the expense of the more complex. They actually make something – more capsules of virus – that is not of itself alive, at the expense of whatever living thing functioned as its host. So that seems to me a good candidate for resistance to the Spirit of God, confessed in the Niceno-Constantinopolitan Creed as 'the Lord, the giver of life'.

I am picturing here a God who applies a certain subtle but ultimately irresistible pressure to the evolutionary process, such that it has a certain gentle overall bias, what Arthur Peacocke called a propensity (Peacocke 1993: 220), towards complexification – not detectable in any individual instance, but only by looking at the system as a whole, and over large time spans. God allows all sorts of behaviours to develop, which include resistance to the divine will such as parasitism and viral infection, though in both cases these may over time turn out to serve God's overall purposes. Parasites may develop into or revert to symbionts; viral genes may be absorbed into host genomes and may have beneficial properties in promoting genetic novelty (Hoggard Creegan 2013: 112–3). Moritz goes much too far when he says simply that viruses are evil (Moritz 2020). A protein of probable viral origin is essential to the development of the human placenta (Schilling 2020). These resistances I am postulating do not ultimately prevail against the overall purposes of God, even though they may add to the burden of creaturely suffering already entailed by a world of evolutionary struggle, the only type of world (so I claim) capable of realising God's purposes in creation.

That is one postulate, which seeks to put flesh on Fiddes' suggestion. A second, much more hazardous step would be to ask: how are we to understand the origin of these resistances, which culminate in the wilful opposition to God's ways with the world that we see in human sin? A number of possibilities occur to me. Those influenced by process theology may simply see the resistance as an aspect of the freedom of created entities. This freedom is intrinsic in strict process metaphysics. Or the freedom may be thought of as a gift of God to creation, resulting in a kind of free-process argument for why God allows it. Creatures on this model are continually responding to God but have always the possibility of resisting. This freedom, at every level of complexity in creation, is taken to be a good in itself. I take this to be the position that Fiddes' sentence implies.

There was an important podcast produced by the US organisation Biologos in the summer of 2020,[45] in which Francis Collins, head of the US National Institutes of Health and himself a Christian author, debated with N. T. Wright, the famous Anglican New Testament scholar, about COVID. Wright held on biblical grounds that there is a certain dark power, which we shall never understand, that has always opposed God's will in creation. Collins, in contrast, produced a kind of package deal argument that there is nothing all good or all bad in biology, and probably there must be the possibility of the bad along with the good, just as the Earth needs earthquakes (and the resultant tsunamis) if it is to be a planet fruitful for life.

I am beginning to wonder if there might not be a sense in which both Wright and Collins might be correct. My initial sympathies were all with Collins. The same processes generate wonderful creaturely characteristics and also great suffering. Even viruses as we have seen can have beneficial effects. But a Christian thinker meditating on the biblical witness, from the serpent in Genesis 3 to the more evident dualisms of the New Testament, cannot help considering whether this element of creaturely resistance we have been exploring, this countering of God's presumed will to complexity and beauty and interdependence, might not have an ultimate origin in a spiritual disaffection pre-dating the creation itself. This is not a necessary component of this exploration, but I still think there is ground worth exploring here.

Of course as soon as one starts to speak in these terms, Milton's *Paradise Lost* looms in the imagination, with its magnificent personifications of rebellious spirits. That is not in my view a helpful direction to take. As Wright says in the podcast, we can never understand, should never try to understand, this spiritual rebellion. It is of its very nature irrational. It is a dereliction from the good rather than a separate power of its own. I have always taken very seriously the existence of this evil tempting the human spirit. Jesus evidently took it seriously in the culminating petitions of the Lord's Prayer. This is why many Christian churches retain their ministry of deliverance. I have tended to take the view that this spiritual evil derives its power and influence from the multiplication of human choices to resist God, and that it has no power over the wider creation. And I would not want to go far in asserting such a power. It cannot be a power comparable with that of the creator of all existents *ex nihilo*. It cannot in my view be a power great enough in comparison to that creator to be the power responsible for the existence of all struggle in creation. Nor is it plausible to regard such a power as responsible for what all biologists recognise as a necessity in organisms, biological death.

---

[45] Available at biologos.org.

But I wonder whether a temptation to resistance, rather than response, to the gentle creative pressure of the Spirit of God, across the whole sweep of creation, might not originate from spiritual resistance to God in realms of reality beyond our imagination.[46] So perhaps the consequences of some freely chosen angelic rebellion, in terms of a temptation of physical creatures towards resisting the direction of God's creative will, can be seen on the margins of the evolving world. Those consequences became intensified when freely choosing creatures evolved capable of conscious worship, and hence also of the worship of idols. The impact of the angelic rebellion gathers to a climax in the battle for the human spirit, a battle Christians confess to have been won on the Cross of Christ. Indeed this speculation I am advancing in relation to the wider creation might be helpful in emphasising the necessity and cosmic reach of the atoning work of Christ (see Section 9).

I want to reiterate that I remain committed to the only-way argument. If you ask me for the one overarching reason why the history of creation is so full of struggle and suffering, that is the sort of answer I would continue to give. The vast preponderance of the struggle and suffering in evolutionary history remains attributable to that same process of evolution by natural selection that has generated such extraordinary creaturely properties, including of course human intelligence. But here and there we may gain hints of the resistance of which Fiddes writes, and the option to think of this as at least catalysed by spiritual influences is open to us, and has some support in scripture and tradition.[47]

Conclusion

This Element has focussed on the suffering of non-human animals, and the problem it poses for monotheisms that postulate an omnipotent, omnibenevolent deity. The problem can be addressed either philosophically or theologically. After some general sounding of territory common to the great monotheisms, and a brief historical survey, a range of contemporary Christian theological responses has been evaluated. Arguments have been presented to support the 'only-way' argument over fall-based or 'free-process' proposals. But broader exploration of the problem reveals the advisability of invoking a combination of responses, to include divine co-suffering and a post-mortem life for animals. Finally, two speculative proposals have been offered, one of which develops the only-way argument, and the other introduces the possibility of including an element of spiritually catalysed resistance to the divine will. I commend this fast-moving and generative set of theological puzzles to the reader's further reflection.

---

[46] There may be a link to be made here with Deane-Drummond's formulation of 'shadow Sophia' as having 'a seductive power over the natural world' (2009: 190).

[47] The suggestion in this section formed part of the 2022 Boyle Lecture, published as Southgate (2022).

References

Adams, Marilyn McCord and Adams, Robert Merrihew. 1990. *The Problem of Evil*. Oxford: Oxford University Press.

Alexander, Denis. 2008. *Creation or Evolution – Do We Have to Choose?* Oxford: Monarch.

Anderson, Gary A. and Bockmuehl, Markus (eds.). 2018. *Creation* ex nihilo, *Origins, Developments, Contemporary Challenges*. Notre Dame, IL: University of Notre Dame.

Aquinas, St Thomas. 2020. *Summa theologiae*. Transl. The Fathers of the English Dominican Province. newadvent.org/summa (accessed September 7 2022)

Attfield, Robin. 2006. *Creation, Evolution and Meaning*. Aldershot: Ashgate. 2017. *Nature, Value and God*. Abingdon: Routledge.

Barbour, Ian G. 2001. God's Power: A Process View. In John Polkinghorne, ed., *The Work of Love: Creation as Kenosis*. London: SPCK, pp. 1–20.

Barth, Karl. 1961. *Church Dogmatics, Vol. 3, Part 3, The Doctrine of Creation*. Trans. G. W. Bromiley and R. J. Ehrlich, ed. G. W. Bromiley and T. F. Torrance. Edinburgh: T&T Clark.

Bauman, Whitney. 2009. *Theology, Creation, and Environmental Ethics: From Creatio Ex Nihilo to Terra Nullius*. Abingdon: Routledge.

Beer, Gillian. 2009. *Darwin's Plots: Evolutionary Narrative in Darwin, George Eliot, and Nineteenth-Century Fiction*. 3rd ed. Cambridge: Cambridge University Press.

Bowker, John. 1970. *Problems of Suffering in Religions of the World*. Cambridge: Cambridge University Press.

Boyd, Gregory A. 2017. *The Crucifixion of the Warrior God*, vol. 2. Minneapolis, MN: Fortress Press.

Brooke, John Hedley. 1991. *Science and Religion: Some Historical Perspectives*. Cambridge: Cambridge University Press.

Burrell, David B., Cogliati, Carlo, Soskice, Janet M., and Stoeger, William R., (eds.). 2010. *Creation and the God of Abraham*. Cambridge: Cambridge University Press.

Burrus, Virginia. 2019. *Ancient Christian Ecopoetics: Cosmologies, Saints, Things*. Philadelphia, PA: University of Pennsylvania Press.

Cherry, Shai. 2011. Judaism, Darwinism, and the Typology of Suffering. *Zygon* 46(2), 317–29.

Clayton, Philip and Knapp, Steven. 2011. *The Predicament of Belief*. New York: Oxford University Press.

Clough, David. 2012. *On Animals: Vol. 1: Systematic Theology.* London: T&T Clark.

Coakley, Sarah. 2001. Kenosis: Theological Meanings and Gender Connotations. In John Polkinghorne, ed., *The Work of Love: Creation as Kenosis.* London: SPCK, pp. 192–210.

2012. Sacrifice Regained: Evolution, Cooperation and God. www.giffordlectures.org (accessed September 5 2022).

2013. Evolution, Cooperation and Divine Providence. In Sarah Coakley and Martin Nowak, eds., *Evolution, Games and God: The Principle of Cooperation.* Cambridge, MA: Harvard University Press, pp. 375–85.

Cobb, John B., Jr, and Griffin, David Ray. 1976. *Process Theology: An Introductory Exposition.* Belfast: Christian Journals.

Conti, Alessandro. 2017. John Wyclif. In *The Stanford Encyclopedia of Philosophy.* www.plato.stanford.edu/John Wyclif (accessed August 14 2022).

Conway Morris, Simon. 2003. *Life's Solution: Inevitable Humans in a Lonely Universe.* Cambridge: Cambridge University Press.

2022. *From Extraterrestrials to Animal Minds: Six Myths of Evolution.* West Conshohocken, PA.: Templeton Foundation Press.

Darwin, Charles. 1856. *Letter to J.D. Hooker of July 13 1856.* Catalogued as Letter No. 1924, www.darwinproject.ac.uk (accessed August 26 2022).

1859. *On the Origin of Species by Means of Natural Selection, or the Preservation of Favoured Races in the Struggle for Life.* London: John Murray.

1860. *Letter to Asa Gray of 22 May 1860.* Catalogued as Letter No. 2814, www.darwinproject.ac.uk (accessed August 26 2022).

Davison, Andrew. 2018. 'He Fathers-Forth Whose Beauty Is Past Change,' but 'Who Knows How?': Evolution and Divine Exemplarity. *Nova et Vetera,* English edition, 16(4), 1067–102.

2020a. 'Biological Mutualism: A Scientific Survey'. *Theology and Science* 18(2), 190–210.

2020b. 'Christian Doctrine and Biological Mutualism: Some Explorations in Systematic and Philosophical Theology'. *Theology and Science* 18(2), 258–78.

Dawkins, Richard. 1983. Universal Darwinism. In Derek S. Bendall, ed., *Evolution from Molecules to Men.* Cambridge: Cambridge University Press, pp. 403–25.

Deane-Drummond, Celia E. 2009. *Christ and Evolution: Wonder and Wisdom.* Minneapolis, MN: Fortress Press.

2018. Perceiving Natural Evil through the Lens of Divine Glory? A Conversation with Christopher Southgate. *Zygon* 53(3), 792–807.

deGrazia, David. 1996. *Taking Animals Seriously: Mental Life and Moral Status*. Cambridge: Cambridge University Press.

Dembski, William A. 2009. *The End of Christianity: Finding a Good God in an Evil World*. Nashville, TN: Broadman and Holman.

Dougherty, Trent. 2014. *The Problem of Animal Pain: A Theodicy for All Creatures Great and Small*. New York: Palgrave Macmillan.

Draper, Paul. 2012. Darwin's Argument from Evil. In Yujin Nagasawa, ed., *Scientific Approaches to the Philosophy of Religion*. Basingstoke: Palgrave Macmillan, pp. 49–70.

Edwards, Denis. 2006. Every Sparrow That Falls to the Ground: The Cost of Evolution and the Christ-Event. *Ecotheology* 11(1), 103–23.

2018. Christopher Southgate's Compound Theodicies: Parallel Searchings. *Zygon* 53(3), 680–90.

Fern, Richard L. 2002. *Nature, God and Humanity: Envisioning an Ethics of Nature*. Cambridge: Cambridge University Press.

Fergusson, David. 2018. *The Providence of God: A Polyphonic Approach*. Cambridge: Cambridge University Press.

Fiddes, Paul S. 1988. *The Creative Suffering of God*. Oxford: Clarendon Press.

2000. *Participating in God: A Pastoral Doctrine of the Trinity*. London: Darton, Longman and Todd.

Garvey, Jon. 2019. *God's Good Earth: The Case for an Unfallen Creation*. Eugene, OR: Cascade Books.

Gould, Stephen Jay. 1989. *Wonderful Life: The Burgess Shale and the Nature of History*. Harmondsworth: Penguin.

Greene, Brian. 2004. *The Fabric of the Cosmos: Space, Time and the Texture of Reality*. Harmondsworth: Penguin.

Gregersen, Niels Henrik. 2001. The Cross of Christ in an Evolutionary World. *Dialog: A Journal of Theology* 40(3), 192–207.

Harrison, Peter. 1989. Theodicy and Animal Pain. *Philosophy* 64(247), 79–92.

Haught, John F. 2004. *Deeper than Darwin: The Prospect for Religion in the Age of Evolution*. Oxford: Westview Press.

2005. The Boyle Lecture 2003: Darwin, Design and the Promise of Nature. *Science and Christian Belief* 17, 5–20.

Hick, John. 1966. *Evil and the God of Love*. London: Macmillan.

Hincks, Adam D., S.J. 2018. What Does Physical Cosmology Say about Creation from Nothing? In Gary A. Anderson and Markus Bockmuehl, eds., *Creation* ex nihilo: *Origins, Developments, Contemporary Challenges*. Notre Dame, IL: University of Notre Dame, pp. 319–45.

Hoggard Creegan, Nicola. 2013. *Animal Suffering and the Problem of Evil*. New York: Oxford University Press.

2018. Theodicy: A Response to Christopher Southgate. *Zygon* 53(3), 808–20.

Illingworth, John R. 1890. The Problem of Pain: Its Bearing on Faith in God. In Charles Gore, ed., *Lux Mundi: A Series of Studies in the Religion of the Incarnation*. 3rd ed. London: John Murray, pp. 113–26.

Jablonka, Eva and Marion J. Lamb. 2014, first published in 2005. *Evolution in Four Dimensions: Genetic, Epigenetic, Behavioral, and Symbolic Variation in the History of Life*, revised ed. Cambridge, MA: MIT Press.

Jonas, Hans. 1996. *Mortality and Morality: A Search for Good after Auschwitz*. L. Vogel, ed. Evanston, IL: Northwestern University Press.

Keller, Catherine. 2003. *Face of the Deep: A Theology of Becoming*. Abingdon: Routledge.

Kenney, John Peter. 2019. *On God, the Soul, Evil and the Rise of Christianity*. New York: Bloomsbury.

Kilby, Karen. 2020. *God, Evil, and the Limits of Theology*. London: T&T Clark.

Kilby, Karen and Rachel Davies (eds.). 2020. *Suffering and the Christian Life*. London: T&T Clark.

Kojonen, E. V. Rope. 2021. *The Compatibility of Evolution and Design*. Cham: Palgrave Macmillan.

Leidenhag, Joanna. 2020. *Minding Nature: Theological Panpsychism and the Doctrine of Creation*. London: Bloomsbury.

Lewis, Clive S. 1962, first published 1940. *The Problem of Pain*. New York: Macmillan.

Lloyd, Michael. 2018a. Theodicy, Fall, and Adam. In Stanley P. Rosenberg, Michael Burdett, Michael Lloyd, and Benno van den Toren eds., *Finding Ourselves after Darwin: Conversations on the Image of God, Original Sin, and the Problem of Evil*. Grand Rapids, MI: Brazos Press, pp. 244–61.

2018b. The Fallenness of Nature: Three Non-Human Suspects. In Stanley P. Rosenberg, Michael Burdett, Michael Lloyd, and Benno van den Toren eds., *Finding Ourselves after Darwin: Conversations on the Image of God, Original Sin, and the Problem of Evil*. Grand Rapids, MI: Brazos Press, pp. 262–79.

2018c. Conclusion to Part 3. In Stanley P. Rosenberg, Michael Burdett, Michael Lloyd, and Benno van den Toren eds., *Finding Ourselves after Darwin: Conversations on the Image of God, Original Sin, and the Problem of Evil*. Grand Rapids, MI: Brazos Press, pp. 326–30.

Loke, Andrew Ter Ern. 2022. *Evil, Sin and Christian Theism*. Abingdon: Routledge.

Mason, Georgia J. and Lavery, J. Michelle 2022. What Is It Like to Be a Bass? Red Herrings, Fish Pain and the Study of Animal Sentience. *Frontiers in Veterinary Science* 9, 788289.

May, Gerhard. 1994. *Creatio ex nihilo: The Doctrine of 'Creation out of Nothing' in Early Christian Thought*, trans. A. S. Worrall. Edinburgh: T&T Clark.

McDaniel, Jay B. 1989. *Of God and Pelicans: A Theology of Reverence for Life*. Louisville, KY: Westminster John Knox Press.

1998. Can Animal Suffering be Reconciled with Belief in an All-Loving God? In Andrew Linzey and Dorothy Yamamoto, eds., *Animals on the Agenda: Questions about Animals for Theology and Ethics*. London: SCM Press, pp. 161–72.

McFague, Sallie. 2020. Jesus the Christ and Climate Change. In Ernst Conradie and Hilda Koster, eds., *The T&T Handbook of Christian Theology and Climate Change*. London: T&T Clark, pp. 513–23.

McGrath, Alister. 2016. *Re-Imagining Nature: The Promise of a Christian Natural Theology*. Chichester: Wiley-Blackwell.

McFarland, Ian A. 2014. *From Nothing: A Theology of Creation*. Louisville, KY: Westminster John Knox Press.

McLaughlin, Ryan. 2014. *Preservation and Protest: Theological Foundations for an Eco-Eschatological Ethics*. Minneapolis, MN: Fortress Press.

Messer, Neil. 2009. Natural Evil after Darwin. In Michael S. Northcott and Robert J. Berry, eds., *Theology after Darwin*. Milton Keynes: Paternoster, pp. 139–54.

2020. *Science in Theology: Encounters between Science and the Christian Tradition*. London: Bloomsbury.

Moltmann, Jürgen. 1990. *The Way of Jesus Christ: Christology in Messianic Dimensions*. Trans. M. Kohl. London: SCM Press.

Moritz, Joshua. 2014. Animal Suffering, Evolution and the Origins of Evil: Toward a 'Free-Creatures Defense'. *Zygon* 49(2), 348–80.

2020. 'Are Viruses Evil?' *Theology and Science* 18(4), 564–78.

Murphy, Nancey. 2007. Science and the Problem of Evil: Suffering as a By-Product of a Finely Tuned Cosmos. In Nancey Murphy, Robert J. Russell, and William Stoeger S.J., eds., *Physics and Cosmology: Scientific Perspectives on the Problem of Evil in Nature*. Vatican City: Vatican Observatory, pp. 131–51.

Murray, Michael J. 2008. *Nature Red in Tooth and Claw: Theism and the Problem of Animal Suffering*. New York: Oxford University Press.

Murray, Michael J. and Greenberg, Sean. 2013. Leibniz on the Problem of Evil. In *The Stanford Encyclopedia of Philosophy*. www.plato.stanford.edu (accessed August 26 2022).

Oord, Thomas Jay. 2015. God Always Creates out of Creation in Love: *Creatio ex Creatione a Natura Amoris*. In Thomas J. Oord, ed., *Theologies of Creation: Creatio ex nihilo and Its New Rivals*. Abingdon: Routledge, pp. 109–22.

Oord, Thomas Jay (ed.) 2015. *Theologies of Creation: Creatio ex nihilo and Its New Rivals*. Abingdon: Routledge.

Page, Ruth. 1996. *God and the Web of Creation*. London: SCM Press.

Peacocke, Arthur. 1993. *Theology for a Scientific Age: Being and Becoming – Natural, Divine, and Human*. London: SCM Press.

    1998. Biological Evolution – A Positive Theological Appraisal. In Robert J. Russell, William R. Stoeger, S.J. and Francisco J. Ayala, eds., *Evolutionary and Molecular Biology: Scientific Perspectives on Divine Action*. Vatican City: Vatican Observatory, pp. 357–76.

    2001. The Cost of New Life. In John Polkinghorne, ed., *The Work of Love: Creation as Kenosis*. London: SPCK, pp. 21–42.

Pedersen, Daniel. 2020. *Schleiermacher's Theology of Sin and Nature: Agency, Value and Modern Theology*. Abingdon: Routledge.

Plantinga, Alvin. 1974. *God, Freedom and Evil*. Grand Rapids, MI: Eerdmans.

Polkinghorne, John. 1989. *Science and Providence: God's Interaction with the World*. London: SPCK.

    1998. *Belief in God in an Age of Science: The Terry Lectures*. New Haven, CT: Yale University Press.

    (ed.) 2001. *The Work of Love: Creation as Kenosis*. London: SPCK.

    2005. *Exploring Reality: The Intertwining of Science and Religion*. London: SPCK.

    2009. Pelican Heaven. *Times Literary Supplement*. April 3, 31.

    2012. Reflections of a Bottom-Up Thinker. In Fraser Watts and Christopher Knight, eds., *God and the Scientist: Exploring the Work of John Polkinghorne*. Aldershot: Ashgate, pp. 1–12.

Ritchie, Sarah Lane. 2019. *Divine Action and the Human Mind*. Cambridge: Cambridge University Press.

Rogerson, John. 1991. Genesis 1–11. Sheffield: JSOT Press.

Rolston, Holmes, III. 1986. *Philosophy Gone Wild: Essays in Environmental Ethics*. Buffalo, NY: Prometheus Books.

    1988. *Environmental Ethics: Duties to and Values in the Natural World*. Philadelphia, PA: Temple University Press.

    1992. Disvalues in Nature. *The Monist* 75, 250–78.

    1994. Does Evolution Need to be Redeemed? *Zygon* 29(2), 205–29.

    2001. Kenosis and Nature. In John Polkinghorne, ed., *The Work of Love: Creation as Kenosis*. London: SPCK, pp. 43–65.

    2006, first published 1987. *Science and Religion: A Critical Survey*. Philadelphia, PA: Templeton Foundation Press.

    2018. Redeeming a Cruciform Nature. *Zygon* 53(3), 739–51.

Rosenberg, Stanley P. 2018. Can Nature be 'Red in Tooth and Claw' in the Thought of Augustine? In Stanley P. Rosenberg, Michael Burdett, Michael Lloyd, Benno van den Toren, eds., *Finding Ourselves after Darwin: Conversations on the Image of God, Original Sin, and the Problem of Evil*. Grand Rapids, MI: Baker Books, pp. 226–43.

Rota, Michael. 2013. The Problem of Evil and Cooperation. In Sarah Coakley and Martin Nowak, eds., *Evolution, Games and God: The Principle of Cooperation*. Cambridge, MA: Harvard University Press, pp. 362–74.

Rowe, William L. 1990. The Problem of Evil and Varieties of Atheism. In Marilyn McCord Adams and Robert Merrihew Adams, eds., *The Problem of Evil*. Oxford: Oxford University Press, pp. 126–37.

Ruse, Michael. 2001. *Can a Darwinian be a Christian? The Relationship between Science and Religion*. Cambridge: Cambridge University Press.

Russell, Robert J. 1998. Special Providence and Genetic Mutation: A New Defense of Theistic Evolution. In Robert J. Russell, William R. Stoeger, S. J. and Francisco J. Ayala, eds., *Evolutionary and Molecular Biology: Scientific Perspectives on Divine Action*. Vatican City: Vatican Observatory, pp. 191–223.

2008. *Cosmology: From Alpha to Omega*. Minneapolis, MN: Fortress Press.

2019. Moving ahead on Christopher Southgate's Compound Only-Way Theodicy. *Theology and Science* 17(2), 185–94.

Russell, Robert J., Stoeger, William R., S. J. and Ayala, Francisco J. (eds.). 1998. *Evolutionary and Molecular Biology: Scientific Perspectives on Divine Action*. Vatican City : Vatican Observatory.

Schilling, Mirjam. 2020. A Virocentric Perspective on Evil. *Zygon* 56(1), 19–33.

Schneider, John R. 2020. *Animal Suffering and the Darwinian Problem of Evil*. Cambridge: Cambridge University Press.

Slootweg, Piet. 2022. *Teeth and Talons Whetted for Slaughter: Divine Attributes and Suffering Animals in Historical Perspective*. Kampen: Summum.

Sollereder, Bethany. 2019. *God, Evolution and Animal Suffering: Theodicy without a Fall*. Abingdon: Routledge.

Southgate, Christopher. 2008. *The Groaning of Creation: God, Evolution and the Problem of Evil*. Louisville, KY: Westminster John Knox Press.

2011a. Re-reading Genesis, John, and Job: A Christian's Response to Darwinism. *Zygon* 46(2), 365–90.

2011b. A Test-Case: Divine Action. In Christopher Southgate, ed., *God, Humanity and the Cosmos: A Textbook in Science and Religion*. 3rd ed. London: T&T Clark, pp. 274–312.

2014. Does God's Care Make Any Difference? Theological Reflection on the Suffering of Non-Human Creatures. In Ernst M. Conradie, Sigurd Bergmann, Celia Deane-Drummond, and Denis Edwards, eds., *Christian Faith and the Earth: Current Paths and Emerging Horizons in Ecotheology*. London: Bloomsbury, pp. 97–114.

2015. God's Creation Wild and Violent, and Our Care of Other Animals. *Perspectives on Science and Christian Faith* 67, 245–53.

2018a. *Theology in a Suffering World: Glory and Longing*. Cambridge: Cambridge University Press.

2018b. 'Free-Process' and 'Only Way' Arguments. In Stanley Rosenberg, Michael Burdett, Michael Lloyd, and Benno van den Toren, eds., *Finding Ourselves after Darwin: Conversations on the Image of God, Original Sin, and the Problem of Evil*. Grand Rapids, MI: Baker Books, pp. 293–305.

2018c. Response with a Select Bibliography. *Zygon* 53(3), 909–30.

2022. God and a World of Natural Evil: Theology and Science in Hard Conversation. (The 2022 Boyle Lecture.) *Zygon* 57(4), 1124–34.

2023a, forthcoming. Values and Disvalues in Creation. In Jason Goroncy, ed., *The T&T Clark Handbook of the Doctrine of Creation*. London: T&T Clark.

2023b, forthcoming. Science and Theodicy. In Matthias Grebe and Johannes Grössl, eds., *The T&T Clark Handbook of the Problem of Suffering and Evil*. London: T&T Clark.

Southgate, Christopher, and Andrew Robinson. 2007. Varieties of Theodicy: An Exploration of Responses to the Problem of Evil Based on a Typology of Good-Harm Analyses. In Nancey Murphy, Robert J. Russell, and William R. Stoeger S.J., eds., *Physics and Cosmology: Scientific Perspectives on the Problem of Evil in Nature*. Vatican City: Vatican Observatory, pp. 67–90.

Surin, Kenneth. 1986. *Theology and the Problem of Evil*. Oxford: Basil Blackwell.

Tanner, Kathryn. 2005. *God and Creation in Christian Theology: Tyranny or Empowerment?* Minneapolis, MN: Fortress Press.

Tilley, Terrence. 1991. *The Evils of Theodicy*. Oxford: Blackwell.

Tooley, Michael. 2019. *The Problem of Evil*. Cambridge: Cambridge University Press.

Van Inwagen, Peter. 1995. *God, Knowledge, Mystery*. Ithaca, NY: Cornell University Press.

2006. *The Problem of Evil: The Gifford Lectures Delivered in the University of St Andrews in 2003*. Oxford: Clarendon Press.

Von Balthasar, Hans Urs. 1994. *Theodrama: Theological Dramatic Theory, Vol IV: The Action*. Trans. G. Harrison. San Francisco, CA: Ignatius Press.

Wahlberg, Mats. 2015. Was Evolution the Only Possible Way for God to Make Autonomous Creatures? Examination of an Argument in Evolutionary Theodicy. *International Journal for Philosophy of Religion* 77, 37–51.

Ward, Keith. 1996. *Religion and Creation*. Oxford: Oxford University Press.

Wesley, John. 1825. The General Deliverance. In *Sermons on Several Occasions, Vol II*. London: J. Kershaw, pp. 121–32.

Whitehead, Alfred North. 1929. *Process and Reality: An Essay in Cosmology*. Cambridge: Cambridge University Press.

Wildman, Wesley J. 2007. The Use and Meaning of the Term 'Suffering' in Relation to Nature. In Nancey Murphy, Robert J. Russell, and William R. Stoeger, S. J., eds., *Physics and Cosmology: Scientific Perspectives on the Problem of Evil in Nature*. Vatican City: Vatican Observatory, pp. 53–66.

Young, Frances. 2013. *God's Presence: A Contemporary Recapitulation of Early Christianity*. Cambridge: Cambridge University Press.

Cambridge Elements ☰

Religion and Monotheism

Paul K. Moser

Loyola University Chicago

Paul K. Moser is Professor of Philosophy at Loyola University Chicago. He is the author of *Paul's Gospel of Divine Self-Sacrifice; The Divine Goodness of Jesus; Divine Guidance; Understanding Religious Experience; The God Relationship; The Elusive God* (winner of national book award from the Jesuit Honor Society); *The Evidence for God; The Severity of God; Knowledge and Evidence* (all Cambridge University Press); and *Philosophy after Objectivity* (Oxford University Press); co-author of *Theory of Knowledge* (Oxford University Press); editor of *Jesus and Philosophy* (Cambridge University Press) and *The Oxford Handbook of Epistemology* (Oxford University Press); co-editor of *The Wisdom of the Christian Faith* (Cambridge University Press). He is the co-editor with Chad Meister of the book series *Cambridge Studies in Religion, Philosophy, and Society.*

Chad Meister

Affiliate Scholar, Ansari Institute for Global Engagement with Religion, University of Notre Dame

Chad Meister is Affiliate Scholar at the Ansari Institute for Global Engagement with Religion at the University of Notre Dame. His authored and co-authored books include *Evil: A Guide for the Perplexed* (Bloomsbury Academic, 2nd edition); *Introducing Philosophy of Religion* (Routledge); *Introducing Christian Thought* (Routledge, 2nd edition); and *Contemporary Philosophical Theology* (Routledge). He has edited or co-edited the following: *The Oxford Handbook of Religious Diversity* (Oxford University Press); *Debating Christian Theism* (Oxford University Press); with Paul Moser, *The Cambridge Companion to the Problem of Evil* (Cambridge University Press); and with Charles Taliaferro, *The History of Evil* (Routledge, in six volumes). He is the co-editor with Paul Moser of the book series *Cambridge Studies in Religion, Philosophy, and Society.*

About the Series

This Cambridge Element series publishes original concise volumes on monotheism and its significance. Monotheism has occupied inquirers since the time of the Biblical patriarchs, and it continues to attract interdisciplinary academic work today. Engaging, current, and concise, the Elements benefit teachers, researched, and advanced students in religious studies, Biblical studies, theology, philosophy of religion, and related fields.

Cambridge Elements ⁼

Religion and Monotheism

Elements in the Series

Monotheism and the Rise of Science
J. L. Schellenberg

Monotheism and Faith in God
Ian G. Wallis

Monotheism and Human Nature
Andrew M. Bailey

Monotheism and Forgiveness
S. Mark Heim

Monotheism, Biblical Traditions, and Race Relations
Yung Suk Kim

Monotheism and Existentialism
Deborah Casewell

Monotheism, Suffering, and Evil
Michael L. Peterson

Necessary Existence and Monotheism: An Avicennian Account of the Islamic Conception of Divine Unity
Mohammad Saleh Zarepour

Islam and Monotheism
Celene Ibrahim

Freud's Monotheism
William Parsons

Monotheism in Christian Liturgy
Joris Geldhof

Monotheism and the Suffering of Animals in Nature
Christopher Southgate

A full series listing is available at: www.cambridge.org/er&m

Printed in the United States
by Baker & Taylor Publisher Services